OHIO NORTHERN UNIVERSITY

THE NEW UNITED NATIONS

A REAPPRAISAL OF UNITED STATES POLICIES

By GEORGE E. TAYLOR AND BEN CASHMAN

The United States must decide how the U.N. fits into its national strategy in its efforts to cope with the unanticipated problems that have arisen since 1945.

This study argues that the United States should regard the new U.N. as one instrument among several for the prosecution of American foreign policy. The eventual consolidation of an international organization effective enough to guarantee the peace should always be our national objective but this may be achieved as much outside as within the present United Nations.

The fact that the U.S. was the principal architect of the U.N. is sometimes forgotten. There was no disagreement among the major sponsors on the principle of their own primacy in the Organization. The major role of the Big Powers was not easily accepted by the smaller nations but there was no choice open to them except to agree to it or not to have an international organization.

The Soviet Union immediately challenged the basic assumptions of the U.N. The belief that the Big Three had common postwar objectives was a myth. The Soviet Union destroyed any real possibility of the Security Council serving as the main U.N. organ for the maintenance of international peace and security. To prevent the U.N. from becoming a dormant international body, the U.S. sponsored, after the outbreak of the Korean War, the Uniting for Peace Resolution, which empowered the General Assembly to exercise a peace-keeping function if the Security Council were deadlocked because of a Soviet veto.

This resolution has assumed even greater significance since 1950 because of the de del and and

The problems of membership have been a particularly troublesome item for the U.N. While there has been a vast increase in membership, it came about only because the U.S. and the Soviet Union agreed to "package deals" which in the view of some "erodes" the principles of the Charter. Unquestionably, the most serious membership problems involve the newly independent states and the Chinese representation question. The Chinese representation issue goes to the heart of the problem of membership (is it conditional?). It involves the character and purposes of the U.N. itself.

One of the most significant, dramatic, and far-reaching developments in the U.N. has been the evolution of the Secretariat. It has been a stormy growth wherein the authority of the Secretary-General has increased from that of a mere administrator to that of a positive executive. This struggle perhaps characterizes as much as anything the deep cleavage between the Communist and non-Communist world.

Achievements are limited in the economic, cultural, social, and humanitarian fields. The U.S. has been the chief financial supporter of the U.N. projects in these fields. The Senate has not supported the humanitarian conventions approved by the General Assembly. A major consideration for the U.S. is to decide whether aid should continue to be essentially bilateral or whether its national interests would best be served by channeling a much larger portion of U.S. economic assistance via U.N. multilateral facilities.

U.S. and Soviet confrontation in the U.N. will continue but

giving the new members a majority in the General Assembly. The great expansion in the size of the U.N. by the admission of former colonial areas has led some of the great powers to urge a "return to the Charter" which means restoring peace-keeping primacy to the Security Council which, in turn, means immobility.

The balance of terror has undoubtedly been another significant factor in the survival of the U.N. Both sides, at least for the moment, wish to control nuclear war. All great powers will probably be nuclear powers in the future and there will be increased attention directed to a restoration of great power dominance, probably to include Communist China in this category.

The American people have generally been favorably disposed to the U.N. Most would agree it is not as effective as it should be but serves a purpose in the total U.S. foreign policy. The U.S. Senate has been especially strong in its support of the U.N. Without congressional financial support the U.N. would long ago have been bankrupt. Also, the Senate has been particularly outspoken in its stand on the subject of Chinese representation. In 1961, three significant resolutions were adopted by the Congress opposing the representation of Peiping in the U.N. It is uncertain what stand the Congress will take should the General Assembly decide to allow the Chinese Communists to gain a seat in that body.

The two major functions of the U.N. are the maintenance of international peace and the achievement of international cooperation in solving problems of an economic, social, cultural, and humanitarian character. In both functions there has been only limited success because no one at San Francisco anticipated the vast increase in U.N. membership, the changing role of the General Assembly, or the impact of the Cold War. The failure of the permanent members of the Security Council to reach agreement on any significant common principles has prevented both the creation of an international military force and any serious efforts to reach a disarmament agreement.

of this organization although it oftentimes appears that the Soviet Union is more concerned with its destruction. The U.N. is one area in which the real struggle for control of the world takes place. To prevent Soviet success within or without the U.N. depends upon the effectiveness of U.S. policies which in the first and last instance rest upon the military might of the United States and its allies.

The U.N. is no substitute for a U.S. policy but it is both an instrument and an objective of U.S. policy. A successful U.S. policy in the U.N. does not depend upon charter revisions, but rather on the cultivation of a consensus based on as large a measure as possible of political and economic homogeneity among those states that have no commitment to the Communist powers. This includes a willingness to use all means short of war to bring about social change or to resolve international conflicts. A pragmatic instrumental approach to the U.N. must be based on political and economic approaches which sharpen the contrast between the two great political and economic systems and seek to bring as much of the non-committed world as possible into an interdependent Western-oriented economic and political system. The problem is to strike the right balance, keeping in mind the importance of building a consensus among as many states as possible. Action must be calculated not in terms of a static model of a U.N. which does not in fact exist but rather in terms of a developmental approach. The task is to construct the political, moral, and economic foundations of a future West-oriented U.N. within the present structure of the old U.N. and in the teeth of strong opposition.

George E. Taylor is Chairman of the Department of Far Eastern and Slavic Languages and Literature and Director of the Far Eastern and Russian Institute of the University of Washington. Ben Cashman is a regular member of the faculty of Shoreline Community College, Seattle, and is a part-time faculty member of Seattle University.

THE NEW UNITED NATIONS

A Reappraisal
of United States Policies

By GEORGE E. TAYLOR and BEN CASHMAN

June 1965

PUBLISHED AND DISTRIBUTED BY THE

AMERICAN ENTERPRISE INSTITUTE
FOR PUBLIC POLICY RESEARCH
WASHINGTON, D.C. 20036

George E. Taylor is Chairman of the Department of Far Eastern and Slavic Languages and Literature and Director of the Far Eastern and Russian Institute of the University of Washington. Ben Cashman is a regular member of the faculty of Shoreline Community College, Seattle, and is a part-time faculty member at Seattle University.

Price $1.00

AMERICAN ENTERPRISE INSTITUTE
For Public Policy Research

THE AMERICAN ENTERPRISE INSTITUTE FOR PUBLIC POLICY RESEARCH, established in 1943, is a nonpartisan research and educational organization which studies national policy problems.

Institute publications take two major forms:

1. LEGISLATIVE AND SPECIAL ANALYSES — factual analyses of current legislative proposals and other public policy issues before the Congress prepared with the help of recognized experts in the academic world and in the fields of law and government. A typical analysis features: (1) pertinent background, (2) a digest of significant elements, and (3) a discussion, pro and con, of the issues. The reports reflect no policy position in favor of or against specific proposals.

2. LONG-RANGE STUDIES — basic studies of major national problems of significance for public policy. The Institute, with the counsel of its Advisory Board, utilizes the services of competent scholars, but the opinions expressed are those of the authors and represent no policy position on the part of the Institute.

CONTENTS

I.

THE UNITED STATES PERSPECTIVE
ON THE UNITED NATIONS

It is always appropriate for Americans to ask themselves whether the United Nations is serving the best interests of the United States. The time has come for a critical appraisal because the U.N. today differs very markedly from the body that was launched in San Francisco in April 1945. During the last 20 years the policies of the Communist states, the rapid liquidation of imperialism, the increase in the number of new states, the pace of the armament race, especially the proliferation of nuclear weapons, and the specific actions of the United Nations itself have all combined to bring about far-reaching changes. We have, in effect, a new United Nations.

Some of the shifts in the world balance of forces are exaggerated in the U.N.; others are not reflected at all. There are many problems, such as over-population, arms control, the widening gap between the rich nations and the poor, which are dealt with, if at all, mainly outside the United Nations. The U.N. has shared only modestly in the keeping of the peace between the great powers; the peace, such as it is, depends on the military superiority of the United States and its allies, and this sort of force cannot be used against another great power in the name of the United Nations. Members of the U.N. have contributed only modestly to its economic, social, and humanitarian functions while carrying out extensive programs of their own. But the U.N. has come to include practically every state in the world, with some

1

important exceptions, and the great have allowed the smaller powers to share in the peace-keeping function. The General Assembly, like the lower house in many a bicameral legislature, has become the noisy voice of the multitude. New forces are at work that are pressing on the U.N. problems which its sponsors have sought to avoid. The United States has to decide how the new U.N. fits into its national strategy.

It is the argument in this study that the policy of the United States towards the new U.N. must be an instrumental one. There is every reason to keep, as an objective of national policy, the eventual consolidation of an international organization effective enough to guarantee the peace. The idea has great potential political appeal. The basis for such an organization, a consensus among the powers, does not at present exist; in fact the divisions have never been greater. Those very divisions, however, have served to force on part of the non-Communist world a degree of cohesion that would otherwise have been unthinkable. It is in those policies and institutional arrangements that were developed in the first instance for defensive purposes that the United States is actually building the foundations—political, military, social, and economic—of a type of international organization in which war between the members is excluded from practical consideration. The strategy is clear; it is to use the U.N. as an additional instrument in the furthering of our national interest, not only in the struggle against communism but also in the building of a more prosperous world, and at the same time build a model for a permanent international organization within the framework of the old. The future of the U.N. will ultimately be decided as much outside as inside that institution.

The U.N. as a Policy Objective

The U.S. Role in the Making of the Charter

It is a political fact that the United States was the chief architect of the United Nations and therefore invested in it a considerable amount of national prestige. The United Nations Charter and Organization reflect the ideas of the United States more than those of any other country. After the Yalta conference President Roosevelt said of the U.N.:

> It spells the end of the system of unilateral action and exclusive alliances and spheres of influence and the balances of power, and all the other expedients which have been tried for centuries—and have failed. We propose to substitute for all these a universal organization in which all peace-loving nations will finally have a chance to join.[1]

[1] Quoted in Ruth B. Russell, *A History of the United Nations Charter* (Washington: The Brookings Institution, 1958), p. 547.

Even though all peace-loving nations were theoretically eligible for member-ship, the U.N. structure reflected existing power relationships by giving primacy to the Big Three.

Not all Americans remember that it was the United States Government that proposed that world peace should be maintained by the "four police-men," as Roosevelt called the United States, the United Kingdom, the U.S.S.R., and eventually, China. France, which had refused to help sponsor the United Nations conference at San Francisco, was later added as a per-manent member of the Security Council. It was quite logical that the United States Government also included in its first draft the idea of the veto, for none of the great powers was willing to cooperate on any other basis than complete freedom of action. Later American criticism of the excessive use of the veto was sound and proper, but there was nothing sinister in the original concept of the veto, and most observers would agree that the United States Senate would never have accepted the Charter if this provision had not been included. There was no disagreement among the Big Three—the United States, the United Kingdom, and the Soviet Union—on the principle of the veto. All of them agreed upon the basic concept of great-power rule. Churchill spoke of a Grand Alliance, and the Soviet Union, though most reluctantly, agreed to cooperate because of the emphasis on the role of the great powers.[2] Against the bitter opposition of Stalin and Churchill, the United States insisted that Nationalist China under the leadership of Chiang Kai-shek should become one of the Big Four. Again, the United States had its way. In view of later developments, it is also well to remember that the United States made it very clear to the smaller powers that they had to accept the domination of the great powers or have no United Nations at all. Mr. Evatt of Australia pointed this out at the time:

> At San Francisco we fought to the very limits of our strength to restrict the individual veto power to due proportions. We knew instinctively the dangers involved. We could not accept the viewpoint that because no great powers had in the past ever voluntarily surrendered or restrict-ed such a right of veto, therefore neither in the present nor in the fore-seeable future should any such power be expected to do so. . . . To me it is a tragedy that at San Francisco we were compelled by the force of circumstances to adopt a charter so rigid. . . .[3]

---

[2] Cordell Hull, *The Memoirs of Cordell Hull,* Vol. II (New York: Macmillan, 1948), p. 1247.

[3] Herbert V. Evatt, *The United Nations* (Cambridge: Harvard University Press, 1948), p. 44.

4

The rigidity of the United States view on the role of the Big Powers was stated clearly by Senator Tom Connally before the subcommittee at San Francisco which was trying to reconcile differences on Security Council voting procedures: "You may go home from San Francisco—if you wish, I cautioned the delegates, and report that you have defeated the veto. . . . But you can also say, 'We tore up the Charter.' At that point I sweepingly ripped the charter draft in my hands to shreds and flung the scraps upon the table." [4]

It has been suggested that President Roosevelt had it in mind, after leaving the Presidency, to become the Secretary-General of the United Nations Organization.[5] He apparently felt that the Big Three plus China must be kept together, and that he was the man to do it. He saw himself as the moderator, arbitrator, and final authority between the others—"It was he who spoke the last word." [6] President Roosevelt has been attacked for not anticipating factors that affected the U.N. such as the growth of nuclear weapons and the vast increase in membership. He alone of the Big Three knew the potential of the bomb, and he was also determined to liberate colonial areas. But of greater significance was his faulty estimate of Soviet policy.

The Myth of Unanimity

The assumptions on which the United Nations was constructed were challenged immediately by the intransigeance of the Soviet Union. It is clear now that even if President Roosevelt had lived and even if he had become Secretary-General, he would have failed to implement the central concept of big-power rule. The Grand Alliance did not keep the peace because the basis for it never really existed, even during the war. The close relationship between the United States and the United Kingdom was not matched by a similar relationship with the Soviet Union. To expect that the Soviet Union was even primarily interested in keeping the peace was a view which, if not limited to President Roosevelt, was certainly not shared by all of his advisers.

A reading of the memoirs of Secretary Hull suggests that this was one of the issues upon which he differed with President Roosevelt. According to Mr. Hull, the U.S. Ambassador to Russia, Averell Harriman, reported in late 1944 that we had at that time sufficient evidence to foresee that if a world organization were established requiring agreement of all permanent members for the consideration of any dispute, regardless of whether or not one of them was involved, the Soviet Government would ruthlessly block consideration by the Council of any question that it thought affected its interests. The Soviet

---

[4] Quoted in Russell, *op. cit.,* p. 738.
[5] John Gunther, *Roosevelt in Retrospect* (New York: Harper, 1950), p. 81.
[6] Robert E. Sherwood, *Roosevelt and Hopkins* (New York: Harper, 1948), p. 789.

5

Government, he added, would also insist that such a matter be settled by the Soviet Union with the other country or countries involved, particularly any disputes with her neighbors.[7] Harriman added that in spite of the Soviet sensitiveness and suspicion of motives and actions, there was nothing to indicate that the Soviet Union had any fear of the antagonism of the world against her policies. In spite of his doubts, however, even Mr. Hull did not fully understand the basic nature of totalitarianism. "Narrow-minded people," he said, "may continue to irritate Russia to a point where she will draw back into extreme isolationism and nationalism. We must use friendly methods."[8]

President Roosevelt was quite clear about Soviet dictatorship. On February 10, 1940, he said: "The Soviet Union, as everybody who has the courage to face the facts knows, is run by a dictatorship as absolute as any other dictatorship in the world."[9] But this was done before the wartime alliance and even then was no indication that he understood totalitarianism. Even if he had understood Communist totalitarianism it would have been difficult, in 1944 and 1945, to take steps openly to oppose it owing to the prevailing sympathy toward a wartime ally. The American people came to believe that the U.S.S.R. recognized the necessity of postwar cooperation, if only because of the threat of a resurgent Germany. Furthermore, at the time Roosevelt died it was assumed that the Soviet Union would be in need of many years of peace for postwar reconstruction and in any case would be no match for the military might of the U.S. There would have been some basis for this view only if the American people had not insisted on the rapid and wholesale demobilization of U.S. forces at the end of the war. Although there was no real collaboration during the war itself,[10] the effort to get the Russians to collaborate apparently led to the hope that postwar collaboration was not out of the question. These hopes and illusions died hard in spite of Stalin's famous speech of February 9, 1946, in which he said that a peaceful international order was impossible under the present capitalist development of world economy and then announced a five-year program for rapid industrial and military expansion on a huge scale. In his diary, James Forrestal reports that Associate Justice William O. Douglas interpreted Stalin's speech as "the declaration of World War III."[11] Winston Churchill read the signals in much the same way in his Fulton, Missouri, speech of March 5, 1946, in which he called for an Anglo-American alliance against the Soviet Union.

[7] Hull, *op. cit.*, pp. 1459-60.
[8] *Ibid.*, p. 1465.
[9] Quoted in William C. Bullitt, *The Great Globe Itself* (New York: Scribner, 1946), p. 5.
[10] John R. Deane, *The Strange Alliance* (New York: Viking Press, 1947), p. 47.
[11] *The Forrestal Diaries*, ed. Walter Millis (New York: Viking Press, 1951), p. 134.

6

The cleavage between the Western and the Soviet view of the world and the U.N. soon became perfectly apparent. In the Soviet-Iranian crisis of 1945-46 the Soviets indicated that they never anticipated that any one of the big powers could be censured by the United Nations.[12] The general attitude of the Soviet Union to the United Nations was crystal clear:

> If the matter under discussion could be exploited to further Soviet foreign policy, or to bring discredit on the United States, Britain, or France, no delegation was more forward in referring to it the United Nations. But if the subject concerned Soviet policy, particularly if criticism of Soviet actions was made or implied, the Soviet delegation would not cooperate; it either withdrew from the debate or applied the veto in the Security Council.[13]

In the United Nations as in other relationships, the democratic states found themselves confronted with a pattern of behavior completely at variance with their own. It was extremely difficult for them to adjust to the fact that the Soviet Union and later Communist China rejected all the customary patterns of diplomatic behavior.[14] To put the matter briefly, "the Soviet Union signed the Charter with a more cynical but also more realistic assessment of the United Nations' capacities and prospects than many of its fellow members. Ideological and power-political considerations—and the experience of earlier years—combined to make the U.N. at best an ancillary instrument of Soviet foreign policy."[15]

The view once very common in the United States that the Soviet Union, after joining the United Nations in good faith, only later became imperialistic, uncooperative, hostile, and unmannerly has no foundation in fact. The Soviet Union has remained perfectly consistent in its basic patterns of behavior all the way through; there has been no sudden change in the character and objectives of Soviet foreign policy. Only the methods have changed. There seems no reason to disagree with Gerhart Niemeyer's view that "Communists live in a world which they *will* essentially hostile to the rest of the world. Consequently, Soviet rationality differs radically from that of the West and bars any mutual intercourse. The relation between the two worlds

---

[12] J. M. Mackintosh, *Strategy and Tactics of Soviet Foreign Policy* (New York: Oxford University Press, 1963), p. 66.

[13] *Ibid.*

[14] Carl J. Friedrich and Zbigniew K. Brzezinski, *Totalitarian Dictatorship and Autocracy* (New York: Praeger, 1961), pp. 58-60.

[15] Alexander Dallin, *The Soviet Union at the United Nations* (New York: Praeger, 1962), p. 25.

is irrational, since premises are neither shared nor compared nor considered relevant to each other, but are conceived in mutual exclusiveness and hostility." [16] "In the language of game theory," writes C. B. Marshall, "Communists and non-Communists are like opponents playing different games by different rules on the same board. The Western game conceives the opponents as 'reasonable men,' oriented to compromise, ready to discuss issues on their merits, to play by rules, to obey the referee. The Communists conceive the opponents as mortal enemies, bent on annihilation, eternally aggressive and treacherous. The only rule of this game is the rule of the jungle: survival and victory by all available means." [17] The dialectics of Soviet policy explain why there has not always been open opposition to the U.N. as an institution. Soviet policy distinguishes between the U.N. as it is now and its ultimate objective of a U.N. under Soviet control. In the meantime the U.S.S.R. often finds the U.N. a useful instrument.

Impact of the New Nations

The intensification of the cold war immediately after the conclusion of World War II was obviously the most important of all the factors affecting the United Nations since its creation. It is still the most important question facing the United States in relation to the U.N. But there was another development, the emergence of the new nations and the attrition of the colonial empires, that has come to affect the character of the U.N. and to pose problems for U.S. policy. The vast increase in U.N. membership, from 51 to 114 [18] as of February 1965 has tended to affect the functioning of the United Nations by de-emphasizing the power of the Security Council and increasing the power of the General Assembly in peace-keeping functions. The big powers can be outvoted. The mere increase in numbers of small nations would have been less significant if it had not been for the Uniting for Peace Resolution, [19] adopted at the initiative of the United States in November 1950. This resolution authorizes the General Assembly to take action for the keeping of the peace at times when the Security Council does not act. The United States took this move in order to circumvent Soviet interference with the conduct of the Korean War when the U.S.S.R. returned to the Security Council in August of 1950 after an absence of seven months. This resolution makes the doubling of the U.N. membership very important because the

---

[16] Gerhart Niemeyer with John S. Reshetar, Jr., *An Inquiry into Soviet Mentality* (New York: Praeger, 1956), p. 49.

[17] Charles Burton Marshall, "Conflict and Consensus in the United Nations," in Jeanne J. Kirkpatrick (ed.), *The Strategy of Deception* (New York: Farrar, Straus, 1963).

[18] See Appendix A for list of U.N. members.

[19] See Appendix B for pertinent extracts of this highly important resolution.

new nations have a majority vote if they can be persuaded to hold together—
a task more difficult than might be assumed.

The U.N. could have been used to sponsor an orderly and systematic
transition from colonialism over a reasonable period of time. The U.N. could
have guaranteed eventual independence to colonial areas and helped to prepare them for self-government. This was not to be. The Soviet Union used
the U.N. to hasten a transition which should have been gradual and to press
for the immediate admission to membership of former colonies which were
in no condition to run their own affairs, let alone assist in running those of
others. Hence the chaos in many of the prematurely independent African
and Asian states, and in the U.N. So pervasive was the climate of opinion
that the U.S. even helped to turn over West Irian to the Indonesians and to
overlook India's use of force to recover Goa; the former victims of imperialism apparently could do no wrong.

The U.N., in turn, has had a considerable influence on the domestic and
foreign policies of the new African states. In his book *Politics in Africa,*
Herbert J. Spiro suggests that the United Nations plays an important role
in Africa's "explosion into international politics." He points out that the
U.N. through its Charter, and the General Assembly through its actions, discredit racial discrimination and make it respectable for dependent peoples
to seek self-government; that the U.N. provides a forum for independence
movements of all colonial areas, including Africa; and that the U.N., unlike
the old League of Nations, assumes a greater responsibility for bringing
independence to its own trust areas. [20]

For one thing, membership in the U.N. has given the African nationalists
an internationalist outlook that ties them to the U.N. The esteem in which
African independence leaders hold the U.N. has led them to forgo some of
the "conventional paraphernalia of state power," and to give a low priority to
territorial expansion. So jealous are the small states of membership in the
U.N. that they resist all efforts to form federations such as, for example, a
federal union of central African republics. [21]

It was the strident tone adopted by the small states that led some of the
great powers to favor a return to the Charter in order to de-emphasize the
role of the General Assembly and the Secretary-General. Lord Home, when
Foreign Minister, said that a great new effort must be made to bring the
United Nations back to the Charter as it was meant to be. The founder
members, he said, "named the great powers as permanent members in the

---

[20] Herbert J. Spiro, *Politics in Africa, Prospects South of the Sahara* (Englewood
Cliffs, New Jersey: Prentice-Hall, 1962), p. 14.
[21] *Ibid.,* p. 21.

expectation that they . . . would deal together with any breach of the peace by the smaller powers."[22] General de Gaulle ridiculed the Assembly meetings: "So that now the meetings of the United Nations are no more than riotous and scandalous sessions where there is no way to organize an objective debate and which are filled with invective and insult proffered especially by the Communists and by those who are allied with them against the Western nations." France, continued de Gaulle, must wait for the day when common sense will again prevail and when the "reasonable nations, noting the results of experience, will wish to resume this great world undertaking on a new basis."[23] What is at stake here is the formulation of a new relationship between the great powers and the weak ones, consequent on the virtual disappearance of the previous imperialist connection.

Since the extension of the principle of one state, one vote, to the many little states, particularly those in Africa, that have been created during the last ten years, some of them hardly above the tribal level in social and political organization, we find the tone and temper of the United Nations approximating that of early American Jacksonian democracy. It is these new conditions that have given rise to the talk about returning to the Charter in order to counteract the widely diffused authority of the General Assembly. It is already clear that if we support the expanding role of the General Assembly, we stand alone among the great powers. On the other hand, a return to the Charter is a return to complete immobility.

The Nuclear Balance

The third important development that has affected the United Nations is the ending of the American atomic monopoly and the proliferation of nuclear power. It is now generally well known that the United States and the Soviet Union have the nuclear capacity to destroy each other. This plain, brutal fact is an oversimplification, but all the refinements of methods and technical competence that vary in each country cannot eliminate the possibility of mutual destruction. The balance of terror, as Churchill called it, has probably had more to do with the survival of the United Nations than any other single factor. This is the one centripetal force of overriding significance. There is a compulsion (on both sides) to control nuclear war. The matter has been put very succinctly by Mr. Andrew Boyd: "The powers of destruction which would be let loose in a new conflict do not permit the envisaging

---

[22] Quoted in Andrew Boyd, *United Nations: Piety, Myth and Truth* (Baltimore: Penguin Books, 1962), p. 31.

[23] Quoted in Raymond A. Moore, Jr., *The United Nations Reconsidered* (Columbia: University of South Carolina Press, 1963), p. 145.

10

of a possible failure" that is, of the United Nations.[24] Again, "the crisis of our time is, quite simply, the impact of twentieth-century destructive power upon the age-old chaos which we are polite enough to call the international situation. It is the impact of invention upon confusion. Invention cannot be undone; our only hope of saving civilization lies, therefore, in finding a means of ending the confusion." [25]

We can anticipate that the definition of "great powers" will tend to coincide with nuclear powers. Hence, possibly, the frantic efforts of France and Communist China to become nuclear powers in their own right, and hence also the refusal of these two countries to sign the nuclear test-ban treaty. An overriding concern for the prevention of nuclear mass destruction may very well lead, when all those who have pretensions to the nuclear club have joined it, to a strong drive to revive the original concept of a great power condominium to rule the world. General de Gaulle's statement of February 1965 called for a revision of the Charter by the five permanent members of the Security Council, substituting Communist China for the National Government, in other words, the nuclear powers. The drive is already under way.

The United States Congress: Support and Reservations

The future of U.S. policy towards the U.N. rests more with the Senate than with any other non-executive body. The record is one of strong, if sometimes critical, support; the Senate, in fact, played a decisive role both in the creation and the development of the United Nations. Senator Arthur Vandenberg took a prominent part in the discussions leading to the formulation of the Charter of the United Nations. Senator Connally introduced the resolution of November 5, 1943, by which the Senate favored creation "at the earliest practicable date of a general international organization, based on the principle of the sovereign equality of all peace-loving states . . . for the maintenance of international peace and security." The Senate ratified the United Nations Charter by a vote of 89 to 2 and authorized United States participation in the new organization. For good or for ill, the Senate also empowered the United Nations to locate its headquarters in the United States and by ratifying the headquarters agreement approved diplomatic status for the representatives of the U.N. while in this country. It was this agreement that made it possible for the Chinese Communists to be invited to the U.N. in 1950. This agreement also makes it possible for nations with whom we do not have diplomatic relations, such as Outer Mongolia and Cuba, to send their representatives to the U.N.

---

[24] Andrew Boyd, *The United Nations Handbook* (New York: Pilot Press, 1946), p. 24.
[25] *Ibid.*, p. 25.

The Congress has also been generous in its financial support, both regular and special, of the United Nations. Without United States backing, the U.N. would long ago have been bankrupt. Nor has the Senate support been limited to the major organs of the U.N., the Security Council, and the General Assembly. It has been generous to the work of the specialized agencies, including even the International Court of Justice, a not inconsiderable achievement. Every President from Woodrow Wilson to Franklin D. Roosevelt had urged, without success, the Senate to authorize U.S. participation in the work of the old World Court, even though we did not belong to the League of Nations. On August 2, 1946, the Senate resolved to accept conditionally the jurisdiction of the International Court of Justice in certain limited areas: the interpretation of a treaty, any question of international law, questions of fact, and questions concerning reparations, provided any other state involved also agrees to submit. The Senate, by this so-called Connally Amendment, also eliminated from the Court's authority any problem of "domestic jurisdiction," as determined solely by the U.S. Presidents Truman, Eisenhower, and Kennedy attempted without success to remove these meaningful reservations.

There is one subject on which the Senate has been unusually outspoken, that of Chinese representation. The resolutions of 1961 show very clearly that the passage of time has not diluted the impact of earlier resolutions. At the same time, there are many people in the United States who may not be aware of the Senate's formal position on this issue. It is well to recall that as recently as 1961 the Congress urged the President to inform it of the implications for U.S. policy in the event that the Chinese Communist representatives were seated in the U.N. If this should happen some members of Congress might wish to suggest that the United States withdraw or lessen its support of the U.N.

The Senate held extensive hearings on the revision of the Charter in 1953 in anticipation of the ten-year requirement for review. If the issue should come up again, the Senate will obviously be deeply involved in Charter revision and as far as the United States is concerned would have the last word. On balance it can be said that the measure of support given by the Senate to the U.N. reflects not so much complete Senate satisfaction with everything that the U.N. has done as "realization that collapse of the U.N. would represent an unthinkable disaster." [26]

---

[26] Alexander Uhl, *The U.S. and the U.N.: Partners for Peace* (Washington, D. C.: Public Affairs Institute, 1962), p. 59.

The American Public: Support and Reservations

The changes that have come over the world and the United Nations have been reflected in the discussion of American policy toward the United Nations that has been going on ever since it was founded. The great body of American opinion, which has always been favorable to the United Nations, tends to accept it as an end in itself. There are also those who are disillusioned and some, opposing the very concept itself, who attack the United Nations as being already a super-government which interferes with United States sovereignty and is in essence a Communist conspiracy to control the world.[27] There is responsible opinion which holds that the U.N. does little to preserve the peace and less to improve world economic conditions. At the same time, there is the other American view that the U.N. is not now but should eventually become an international government based on the rule of law. Although the late President Kennedy had an instrumental approach to the United Nations, he foresaw the future in these terms, as he indicated in his State of the Union Message of January 14, 1963: "Today the United Nations is primarily the protector of the small and the weak, and the safety valve for the strong. Tomorrow it can form the framework for a world of law—a world in which no nation dictates the destiny of another, and in which the vast resources now devoted to destructive means will serve constructive ends." This point of view has been carefully worked out and thoroughly documented by Grenville Clark and Louis V. Sohn in their book *World Peace through World Law*. In this view, the United Nations would be a body with sufficient inherent power to thwart individual national wills. The most ardent supporters wish to change it into a genuine world government with binding legislative, executive, and judicial authority.

The ambivalence of these views has been well summarized by Ernest A. Gross:

> It is observable that some in our country who assail the United Nations as a menacing "super state" are often first to deride it for not acting like one in situations of particular moment to the United States. On the other extreme are those who make vague appeals for "support to the United Nations," thus claiming for it an abstract or corporate existence it does not in fact possess.[28]

The official American view which reflects the main body of American opinion is one of support for the United Nations. It is the fourth of the five

---

[27] Robert Welch, *The Blue Book of the John Birch Society* (Belmont, Mass.), pp. 29-30.

[28] Ernest A. Gross, *The United Nations: Structure for Peace* (New York: Harper, 1962), p. 63.

goals of United States foreign policy as outlined by the Department of State. The fourth goal is "to assist in the gradual emergence of a genuine world community, based on cooperation and law, through the establishment and development of such organs as the United Nations, the World Court, the World Bank and Monetary Fund, and other global and regional institutions; that is, a world 'community under law.'" This view was supported by President Johnson when he appeared before the Eighteenth General Assembly: "The greatest of human problems, and the greatest of our common tasks, is to keep the peace and save the future. . . . And more than ever we support the United Nations as the best instrument yet devised to promote the peace of the world and to promote the well-being of mankind." This is not too far from a responsible Republican statement made at Hershey, Pennsylvania, August 21, 1964, which probably comes close to describing the operational code of the U.S. Government: "And while the U.N. was never designed to be a substitute for a clear and resolute U.S. foreign policy, we must take all reasonable steps to help the U.N. become a more effective instrument for peace among nations."

Recent addresses by members of the Department of State revolve around several themes. The first is that the world must be made safe for cultural diversity that permits differences but also permits cooperation. This is in opposition to the Communist idea of a universal dogma. Second, although World War II is over, the conflict continues, with a former ally. Third, as nuclear war is unthinkable there is no alternative to a peace-making organization such as the U.N. Fourth, the main question is how, not why, the U.N. should operate. While the U.N. has never been able to operate as its founders hoped, runs the argument, it has been of more value to the U.S. than to the U.S.S.R. because the U.S. is really interested in diversity and pluralism, whereas the Soviet Union wants a monolith. If the U.N. has not brought the great powers together, it has at least helped to keep them from each other's throats. The Department of State, according to its spokesmen, sees the U.N. as an instrument of policy.

There are two main lines of criticism of the U.N. One is that it does too much, and the other that it does too little. Those who feel that it has done too much think that it has interfered in situations such as the Congo and Suez which they believe would have been better left alone; that it has sponsored and facilitated political movements, such as the anti-colonialism resolutions which are inimical to our interests; that it has provided a forum for the opposition to put pressures on American opinion and therefore policy; and that its economic and technical aid has been ill-conceived and poorly executed. The views of those who feel that the United States Government places too much emphasis on the United Nations as a cornerstone of American policy were forcefully stated by Senator Henry Jackson in his speech to the National Press Club in Washington, D.C., on March 20, 1962. There seems to be good reason to believe, with him, that "the steadying majority of the American people have a more balanced view of the United Nations, and see it for what it is: an aspiration and a hope, the closest approximation we have to a code of international good conduct, and a useful forum of diplomacy for some purposes. The United Nations is, and should continue to be, an important avenue of American foreign policy." The United States should use but not rely upon the U.N.; it is an avenue not a cornerstone.

Many Americans think that the U.N. should be supported as an end in itself. To them it is both an ideal and a hope for unity in a divided and dangerous world. Because they believe that democracy can regenerate the world without coercion they are attracted by legal or institutional gadgetry. They optimistically look to democracy and national self-determination as twin sources of international peace and order, believing that, "the certainty of progress is waiting at the other end of a charter, a constitution, or a court judgment. The United Nations emerges in the minds of some of its American champions as an organization that may confidently be expected to do away with alliances, balance of power, secret diplomacy, and state rivalries." [29] These views tend to characterize those who feel that the U.N. has not done enough either to keep the peace or to assist in the economic growth of the underdeveloped parts of the world. Yet these vague and unrealistic ideas, so widely held, help to explain the curious lack of sound operational doctrine in foreign aid, whether bilateral or multilateral.[30]

The mere existence of a U.N., especially one with headquarters on American soil, raises men's hopes for peace; the institution has a momentum of its own; it has become a subject for both study and propaganda in the schools; it has a measurable influence on public attitudes—attitudes which affect our policymakers and which are taken into account by our opponents. The U.N. is clearly a vital part of American life, both public and private. Its future is a matter of widespread public concern. Since 1945 the world has been changed by a scientific and technological revolution, the emancipation of former colonial peoples, the "revolt against misery," and the collapse of big-power unity. It may be useful, therefore, to review what was established at San Francisco in 1945 and how it has evolved since that time.

---

[29] See Kenneth W. Thompson, *Christian Ethics and the Dilemmas of Foreign Policy* (Durham, N. C.: Duke University Press, 1959), p. 79.

[30] For a useful discussion, see Edward C. Banfield, *American Foreign Aid Doctrines* (Washington, D. C.: American Enterprise Institute, 1963).

II.

THE PEACE-KEEPING FUNCTION

The maintenance of international peace and security is one of the main purposes of the United Nations. To accomplish this, the members agreed to solve all international disputes by peaceful means and to cooperate in solving worldwide problems in the economic, social, cultural, and humanitarian fields. The Charter's principles and purposes and organizational structure were drafted by the big powers, amended by the small powers, and adopted by 51 nations as an imperfect compromise but a workable device for the maintenance of peace. It was the small powers at San Francisco that inspired the eloquent language in the preamble to the Charter.

President Roosevelt, who made the establishment of the U.N. a main objective of U.S. policy, insisted that the organization be established before the conclusion of the war. This was in order to free the United Nations of any responsibility for the postwar settlement. The making of the peace treaties at the end of World War II was not a mission of the United Nations; it was the responsibility of the victorious Allies, who at that time were concerned with the problem of precluding the resurgence of Germany and Japan. It was assumed that the Big Three would rapidly and jointly conclude peace treaties with Japan and Germany, and that these treaties would result in a viable territorial settlement—everybody and everything would be in their places. It was at this point that the United Nations was to assume full responsibility for the maintenance of peace. The failure to conclude joint

15

peace treaties contributed in no small measure to the early difficulties of the United Nations, which found itself trying to reconcile differences among members of the Security Council itself. There are those who feel that some of these problems might have been handled more successfully by the United States if there had never been a United Nations. Certainly if there had been a correct assessment of the nature of Soviet society and foreign policy in 1944, the organization of the U.N. might well have been very different. Such speculation is academic at this time, but it is necessary to remind ourselves that the U.N. was not expected to resolve the problems of peace-making after World War II, nor was it organized in a way to achieve such objectives.

The Members: Rights and Responsibilities

Responsibility for the maintenance of peace was to be shared by the Security Council, which had the primary but not the sole responsibility, and the General Assembly. The Charter obligation required all members of the U.N. to refrain from resorting to "the threat or use of force" in their international relations and to solve all disputes by peaceful means (Article 2). The United Nations, it is well to recall, has no specific authority to compel its members to follow these rules; it is a solemn requirement of membership. According to the Charter, violators are subject to sanctions varying from economic sanctions to direct military action against an aggressor. Very relevant today is the provision in the Charter for the expulsion of members who continuously violate it. When this point was being discussed at San Francisco, the Soviet Union insisted that it would be "unfortunate" to allow a persistent violator to remain a member of the U.N. As the veto, however, applies to the Charter provision for the expulsion of such violators, the Soviet Union can veto its own expulsion. In fact, it was the Soviet Union that insisted upon the application of the veto in such cases because the Soviet Union had not forgotten that it was the only nation ever expelled from the League of Nations. So strongly did the Soviet Union feel on this point that in the early years it blocked the admission of several smaller countries—for example, Portugal—which had voted in the League of Nations for its expulsion.

Domestic Jurisdiction

The Charter would probably never have been accepted if it had not guaranteed to the members, particularly the most powerful ones, complete freedom of action in all matters which they considered to be of domestic concern. Each nation is guaranteed that nothing in the Charter "shall authorize the United Nations to intervene in matters which are essentially within the domestic jurisdiction of any state, or shall require the members to submit such matters to settlement under the present charter." This article has been frequently used—and not only by the Soviet Union. What constitutes "interference" and "domestic jurisdiction" is subject to as many interpretations as there are members of the organization. The Charter provision regarding domestic jurisdiction has complicated the solution of many problems, especially colonial questions. France, for example, refused to accept U.N. discussion of the Algerian problem on the grounds that this was a domestic issue. Portugal insisted that its troubles in Angola and Mozambique were domestic problems on the grounds that these were provinces of Portugal, not colonies. The Soviet Union's official attitude on the Hungarian revolt was to claim that the revolt was a problem entirely for Hungary to settle by itself. Soviet objections to U.N. action in the Congo are based on the allegation that U.N. forces are being used illegally to separate competing Congolese forces and are therefore interfering with the internal affairs of that country. Certain Southern senators in the United States have objected to U.N. discussions on human rights as a possible prelude to U.N. interference in the civil rights problem, such as the U.N. has attempted in the Union of South Africa.

The problem of domestic jurisdiction, in the view of Mr. Clark Eichelberger, a strong supporter of the United Nations, poses the following question: "Is the United Nations the foundation of international policy or an instrument which nations can use or reject as short-sighted self-interest dictates?"[1] In other words, Mr. Eichelberger disapproves of what he considers to be the abuse of the domestic jurisdiction clause of the Charter, particularly by the great powers, in order to further in a short-sighted manner, their own national self-interest. Experience has shown that it is easier for the great powers than for the small to invoke the domestic jurisdiction clause in order to avoid embarrassing questions.

Sovereign Equality

The domestic jurisdiction clause would have made little sense without Article 2 of the Charter, according to which "the Organization is based upon the sovereign equality of all its members." All members, including the Soviet Union, agreed to this provision, which is entirely a product of the Western concept of the nation-state. This provision is both troublesome and misleading. The sovereign equality of states is a juridical concept. Mr. Roosevelt's original concept of the three policemen who would maintain

---

[1] Clark M. Eichelberger, *U.N.—The First Fifteen Years* (New York: Harper, 1960), p. 125.

world order, and the Charter provision for the possession of the veto by five powers only, were a reflection of political realities. The Soviet Union, which neither in theory nor in practice has any use for the concept of the sovereign equality of states, could agree to this provision of the Charter for obvious tactical reasons. A literal application of the provision for the sovereign equality of states permits any member to have a legitimate way out of any international action with which it disagrees.

Some observers insist that most of the difficulties in the way of securing the peaceful settlement of disputes come from what they call the absolute sovereignty of every member of the Organization. Absolute sovereignty is apparently equated with sovereign equality. Andrew Boyd, a British writer for *The Economist* and participant in United Nations affairs, has made this point:

> International anarchy is due to the theory of the absolute sovereignty of the nation-state. A nation which holds this theory not only refuses to tolerate any interference in its private affairs but reserves absolute freedom of action in its relations with other nations; and "freedom of action" naturally includes freedom to make war. Yet no sovereign state would permit its individual citizens, or any group of them, so much as to claim a tithe of the absolute freedom of action which it automatically demands for itself. Indeed, the survival of absolute sovereignty in an age in which the individual citizen is bound to his particular community by stronger economic and social ties than ever before is one of the supreme paradoxes of our time.[2]

A logical conclusion of this argument is that world peace can only be established through the surrender of sovereignty and acceptance of a rule of law.

Without Article 2 (1) of the Charter, there would have been no United Nations. All of the major powers favored it and all of the smaller states insisted on it in the General Assembly. The United States Senate would not have ratified the Charter without it. Although it is true that the United Nations has taken actions that might suggest a weakening of the idea of sovereignty, the record shows that its peace-keeping efforts have more often been persuasive than compulsive. The Soviet Union, it is true, withdrew from Iran in 1946, possibly in response to the firm stand taken by President Truman as well as for its own good reasons; but no United Nations force pushed it out nor was any such action contemplated.[3] The United Nations went into

---

[2] See Boyd, *United Nations Handbook, op. cit.*, p. 9.

[3] Stephen D. Kertesz, "Diplomacy in the Atomic Age: Part II," *The Review of Politics*, April 1959, pp. 364-65.

Korea at the request of the Republic of Korea and after the United States had made it clear that it would intervene regardless of what action might or might not be taken by the United Nations. U.N. intervention did not prevent the Chinese Communists from exercising their "sovereign" right to intervene. The British, French, and Israelis agreed to a United Nations Emergency Force (UNEF) at the time of the Suez crisis; no military force was assembled to be used against these three powers. United Nations intervention in the Congo came about as a result of a request from the government of that country. When Hungary refused to permit the Secretary-General to enter the country, nothing could be done about it except for U.N. resolutions condemning the suppression of the revolt. No U.N. forces went to Cyprus until Archbishop Makarios agreed to have them come. In other words, if a sovereign nation-state has appeared to tolerate or accept United Nations action which interfered with sovereignty, that action was approved in advance by the government concerned. Otherwise, no action was taken at all.

Majority Rule and Financial Responsibility

Refusal to accept majority rule is a further attribute of sovereignty as understood by most members of the U.N. The General Assembly, for example, has been unable to compel its members to pay for what they had previously authorized by a majority vote. The most flagrant cases of nonpayment of assessments have to do with United Nations emergency operations in the Middle East (UNEF) and in the Congo (ONUC). Even the regular budget assessments are not met by all members. The United States pays for one-third of the total regular budget, the other members of the Big Five pay for one-third, and the rest is divided among all the other members. Only 27 of the then full membership of 99 had paid the 1960 assessments for the cost of UNEF and ONUC by September 1961.[4] France and the Soviet Union have declared that they have no intention of paying their shares of these emergency assessments. It was not until October 1964, that the Government of the Republic of China made up enough of its arrears on both regular and emergency payments to avoid the penalties of Article 19. On the record it appears that there has been a greater fear of collapse of the United Nations from bankruptcy due to default by three members of the Big Five than from the impact of the new states' failure to keep the peace. The General Assembly is empowered by Article 19 to deprive a member of

---

[4] John G. Stoessinger, "Financing the United Nations," *International Conciliation,* March 1962, p. 31.

its vote in the Assembly if it is in arrears for more than two years. The International Court of Justice in a non-binding advisory opinion has ruled that special assessments are obligatory on all members.[5] There is no way, of course, that the Court can collect from defaulting nations, nor for that matter can the General Assembly. Defaulting nations suggest that the "aggressors" should pay for the special assessments—Britain, France, and Israel in the case of UNEF, and Belgium in the case of ONUC.

There has been reluctance to invoke Article 19 for fear that the Soviet Union and other affected states will withdraw from the Organization or surrender their votes in the Assembly rather than accept their responsibilities under the Charter. The United States, in October 1964, circulated a memorandum to all members of the United Nations urging that Article 19 be invoked against all defaulting states.

The United States memorandum insisted that the General Assembly should decide on its opening day what to do about those nations which are in arrears on payment of special assessments. In the American view the General Assembly should deprive such nations of their vote until payment is made. The United States cautioned it was not seeking a "confrontation" with the Soviet Union but emphasized that Article 19 must be applied even against a great power. The Soviet Union owed $52.6 million as its share of special assessments for the United Nations force in the Congo and in the Middle East.[6] Six members of the Soviet bloc and Paraguay, Uruguay, and Yemen are in default and subject to the loss of their vote. As France had failed to pay her share of the Congo expenses by January 1, 1965, she automatically endangered her vote in the General Assembly.

The Soviet Government quickly responded to the United States challenge and declared the latter "was intent upon destruction of the United Nations through insistence upon payment of arrears." In the Soviet view the operations of the United Nations which necessitated these special assessments are illegal since they were initiated by the General Assembly and not by the Security Council. The Russian delegate to the Security Council stated that the Soviet Union would not change its position on the issue and it would pay "not one kopeck, not one cent" toward these illegal assessments. The circulation of the United States memorandum was, in the Soviet view, "a new and provocative act by the United States." [7]

The Soviet argument that the demanded payments are illegal because they were not ordered by the Security Council is invalid. The Charter in Article

[5] Moore, op. cit., pp. 151-58.
[6] New York Times, October 9, 1964, pp. 1 and 5.
[7] New York Times, October 10, 1964, pp. 1 and 4.

17 gives to the General Assembly *alone* the power to consider and approve the budget of the organization. The U.N. action in the Congo and the budget for such operations were approved by the General Assembly. The situation is complicated by the fact that France is also unwilling to pay. At the Nineteenth General Assembly "confrontation" was avoided by adoption of the device of "acclamation" without voting and then by adjournment, on February 18, 1965, until September of the same year.

The Security Council: Cockpit of the Powers

The Security Council has been more often the cockpit of the powers than an instrument for peaceful cooperation. When there is unanimity it can be, as many people hoped it would be, a powerful instrument for the keeping of the peace. It can also take the strains of violent international struggle and conflict. In a very real sense the Security Council may be keeping the peace more in its second function than in its first. It is still the most important organ of the United Nations, the only international institution in which the major contenders in the cold war, except for Communist China, have permanent membership. They can walk out but they cannot be ejected; and they are always on call. For the stresses and strains of the cold war the Security Council provides not only a ready-made institution for national confrontations, but also a moral and intellectual framework for the discussion of issues. It has proved to be viable because it was designed to take any kind of strain, including the strain of a complete refusal to cooperate by any one of its permanent members.

It may be well to remind ourselves of the assumptions on which the Security Council was set up. The Charter did not establish a world government, nor was the subject ever discussed. Based on the realities of world power, the Charter recognizes that there are states which are more powerful than others and have a greater capacity for violating the peace, and therefore a greater responsibility for keeping it. There was nothing wrong with the assumption that the Big Five, having a monopoly of power—political, economic, and military—could, if they worked in concert, make it impossible for any state or combination of states to commit aggression. There was no discussion at Teheran of the possibility that an offending aggressor might be one of the big powers, but Secretary of State Edward Stettinius brought the subject into the open when he transmitted the U.N. Charter to the Senate for ratification:

> I submit that these five nations, possessing most of the world's power to break or preserve peace, must agree and act together if peace is to be maintained, just as they had to agree and act together in order to

make possible the United Nations victory in this war. The question is asked: What would happen if one of the five permanent members used the unanimity rule to veto enforcement against itself? The answer is plain. If one of these nations ever embarked upon a course of aggression, a major war would result, no matter what the membership and voting provisions of the Security Council might be.[8]

Unlike other organs of the United Nations, the Security Council has the capacity to make decisions and, if there is unanimity, to enforce them without requiring either the participation or the consent of any other members of the U.N. Because the measures that the Security Council is entitled to take against an aggressor are so severe, no member of the Big Five could agree to a charter which would permit them to be used against itself. It is possible under the Charter for the Security Council to engage in a very wide variety of measures against an aggressor state. These may be the peaceful measures of Article 41 or the warlike measures of Article 42, which include "demonstrations, blockade, and other operations by air, sea, or land forces of members of the United Nations." That is why the veto power belongs to those who are supposed to have the greatest responsibility for the preservation of peace.

The veto was a recognition of the fact—assumed to be basic at the time—that there could be no collective action by the United Nations without the approval of all the great powers. The small powers, somewhat reluctantly, accepted their subordination to the Security Council and continued to support it. Prime Minister Lester Pearson of Canada, a distinguished supporter of the United Nations, speaking ten years after its inauguration said:

> . . . in San Francisco, the smaller powers paid a price, by making certain concessions, for a foundation for the United Nations which we hoped would be solid, but which certainly proved to be illusory. That foundation was to be great power cooperation, and the price we paid was to give these powers a special position under the Charter. We could not have had the United Nations at all without paying this price. It was not too high, and it should not be made an excuse for our failures. The veto . . . is not the cause . . . so much as the reflection, the result of these failures.[9]

Mr. Pearson was right in saying that the great power cooperation was illusory, although there have been one or two occasions on which the Security

---

[8] Quoted in *The United Nations—Its Record and Its Prospects* (New York: Carnegie Endowment for International Peace, 1950), pp. 16-17.

[9] Lester B. Pearson, *The Four Faces of Peace* (New York: Dodd, Mead, 1964), p. 104.

Council acted unanimously, such as the initial intervention in the Congo and in Cyprus. Events since 1945, however, have also shown the assumption to be erroneous that no collective action could be taken without unanimity. Collective action has been taken by the U.N. and it has generally been less than unanimous.

The Security Council's lack of unanimity was fully reflected in the ineffectiveness of its Military Staff Committee, authorized by Article 47 "to advise and assist on all questions relating to the Security Council's military requirements for the maintenance of international peace and security, the employment and command of forces placed at its disposal, the regulation of armaments, and possible disarmament." The effectiveness of this committee, representing the five permanent council members, has been well described by Andrew Boyd:

> Solemnly, every year since then, the Big Five have appointed to the committee a glittering array of top brass—U.S. Air Force generals, Soviet colonel generals, Chinese lieutenant generals, French contre-amiraux, British air vice-marshals. Officially, these stars sing together fortnightly throughout the year. In practice, behind the nameplate there is a deep silence.[10]

Put very briefly, the Big Five have been unable to agree on how to place their forces at the disposal of the United Nations on a unanimous basis. On no occasion has the Military Staff Committee served as the "strategic director" serving under Security Council directions, which is what it was supposed to do. The Military Staff Committee had nothing to do with the conduct of the Korean War, in which the forces of the United States, the United Kingdom, and France, but not China and the Soviet Union, were engaged in carrying out the resolutions of the General Assembly. Far from being a unanimous action, this was very close to war by proxy between the Soviet Union and the other members of the Big Five.

Except in the case of Korea, the military burden of carrying out the subsequent decisions of the U.N. has fallen upon the small powers such as Australia, Canada, Denmark, Ethiopia, Finland, India, Ireland, Morocco, Norway, and Sweden. These countries have actually complied with Article 43 of the Charter, which obligates them to make forces available, on call, for the maintenance of international peace and security. Canada maintains a military unit on call of the Security Council, fully inoculated and prepared to move at a moment's notice to any part of the world. U.N. forces have been used in the Middle East (Palestine and Egypt), Cyprus, and the Congo.

---

[10] See Boyd, *United Nations: Piety, Myth and Truth, op. cit.,* p. 48.

But in no circumstances have U.N. military forces taken direct action against any member of the Big Five. In the case of Suez, the United Kingdom and France gave their consent to the establishment of the United Nations Emergency Forces as a buffer between Egyptian forces and the Anglo-French forces. The United Nations does not have the permanent military forces that it was originally intended to have.

The Soviet Union, which has consistently opposed the creation of any force over which it would not have veto power, in 1960 added the further condition that the office of Secretary-General be replaced by a "troika." More recently the Soviet view has been modified in favor of the creation of a U.N. force drawn solely from members other than the Big Five. If the suggestion can be taken seriously, such a force could now be created on the understanding that it could take action only against the smaller members of the U.N. The modified Soviet position takes into account what has happened. The failure of the Military Staff Committee to agree on the creation and use of military forces shifted the primary responsibility to the small powers and the Secretary-General. The increasingly important role of the Secretary-General has developed what has been called a "U.N. presence"— which often means no more than the presence of one or two men in troubled areas.

One reason perhaps why the Big Five have been willing to permit the creation of small U.N. forces to be used against small nations was to prevent the escalation of a "brush fire war" into a major conflict that would involve the Big Five. Because the two super powers, the United States and the Soviet Union, have a common interest in preventing the development of any conflicts either between small powers or between themselves that might lead to mutual nuclear destruction, they find the United Nations an instrument for communication and action.

What many have thought of as a weakness in the Charter may very well be one of its greatest strengths. If the Charter had been written in such a way (that is, without the veto) that the policemen would have been compelled institutionally and formally and by majority rule to police each other, the organization would have long since ceased to exist. The control of policemen by other policemen takes place in the general arena of power politics, sometimes through war by proxy and only incidentally in the organs of the United Nations. If the policemen cease to behave like policemen, they are not breaking the law, they are merely violating an agreement to undertake joint action for certain purposes, an agreement which they are as free to unmake as to make. The history of the United Nations would have been different indeed if the Big Five had been united in purpose, resolute in action, and blessed with the judgment of Solomon. But they were not. When their internal divisions led to a modest increase in the role of the small powers, they reacted in different ways, some of them calling for a return to the Charter in order to block this trend. Any tendency for the smaller powers to play a larger role in decision-making certainly raises a serious issue for United States policy. Is it better to stick to the Charter even with two sets of policemen controlling one set of small policemen, or to support the trend toward more responsibility for the smaller powers than the Charter envisaged? Part of the problem revolves around the role of the General Assembly.

The Peace-Keeping Record

The record in keeping the peace shows that the U.N. can be useful in preventing the outbreak of small wars or in limiting their scope, and that on rare occasions it can assist in negotiating a settlement of major confrontations between the "policemen." It is a useful, perhaps an essential, barometer of the general state of world opinion, particularly at times of crisis; there is no other permanent clearinghouse for worldwide diplomatic discourse (though not all agree that a clearinghouse is necessary). The U.N. supplements the regular methods of international diplomacy. As the U.N. by definition, however, cannot keep the peace between the "policemen," the main peace-keeping job of opposing the aggression of the Communist world has depended on the military might of the U.S. and its allies.

The International Court of Justice

The peace-keeping record owes little if anything to the International Court of Justice. The writers of the U.N. Charter, more implicitly than explicitly, placed considerable emphasis on respect for and adherence to international law as a means of maintaining international peace and security. They established the International Court of Justice (ICJ) as the "principal judicial organ of the United Nations." The ICJ, which is one of the six principal organs of the United Nations, was never intended to be the only means for the peaceful settlement of disputes. Article 33 lists negotiation, enquiry, mediation, conciliation, arbitration, judicial settlement, resort to regional agencies or arrangements, or other peaceful means. All members of the United Nations are automatically parties to the Statute of the ICJ, but they do not automatically accept its jurisdiction. Article 39 merely makes it possible for members to use the Court if they so wish; its jurisdiction extends only to those cases where parties to the dispute accept its authority. Article 36 of the Court's statute gives it enough authority to cover virtually any international legal dispute which might arise, but this authority is still-born unless nations voluntarily agree to submit disagreements to this tribunal. U.N. members may "declare that they recognize as compulsory *ipso facto* and without special agreement" the jurisdiction of the Court in disputes involving interpretations of a treaty, any question of international law, determination of facts, and the nature and extent of reparations. Some 39 nations have filed declarations subjecting themselves in varying degrees to the Court's jurisdiction.[11] The only permanent member of the Security Council which has not filed such a declaration is the Soviet Union. It is not surprising that the record of the ICJ is one of a limited number of judgments and advisory opinions. Any suggestions for improvement must obviously wait upon the emergence of international relations very different from those now prevailing.[12] The real problem is that there is no consensus among the members of the U.N. on the substance of international law. The ICJ and the U.N. are based on the values of Western civilization which are not accepted by the Communist powers or understood by the Afro-Asian nations.

Regional Security Pacts

Regional security arrangements, such as NATO and SEATO, which are part of that military effort, are registered with the U.N. and are in accord with the Charter. They are in addition to the peace-keeping activities of the U.N. but do not depend on it. It may be well to clear up some common misconceptions about the regional security pacts, which are considered by some not to be in the spirit of the Charter. The Charter is explicit; regional pacts merely have to be reported to the Security Council *ex post facto*. At San Francisco the United States, which had just signed the Act of Chapultepec and had no intention of being forced to renounce it, insisted on Chapter VIII of the Charter, Regional Arrangements, in which regional security pacts are authorized. The Latin American countries were also most anxious to have autonomous regional agreements not dependent upon prior authorization from the Security Council. The Arab nations, Australia, and New Zealand also pressed in the same direction. The Soviet Union did not oppose regional pacts *per se* but wanted all regional actions to be subject to the prior approval of the Security Council, where the veto would be operative. Mr. Churchill, who, like Mr. Roosevelt, originally preferred and actually advocated organization of the world on the basis of regional groupings, held together by the three policemen, went along with the U.S. when it began to

---

[11] *World Peace Through the Rule of Law,* Working Paper for the First World Conference, Athens, Greece, June 30-July 6, 1963, p. 53.

[12] See Wolfgang Friedmann, *The Changing Structure of International Law* (London: Stevens and Sons, 1964), pp. 368-89.

push for a strong international organization because he was willing to accept the U.S. position, however unrealistic he thought it to be, in order to ensure that the U.S. would not withdraw from European affairs.[13]

Regional security pacts are therefore legitimate devices under the Charter; since the right of self-defense is guaranteed to every member, these pacts can be justified in those terms. Some countries regard regional security arrangements such as NATO and SEATO as more important cornerstones of their foreign policy than any of the arrangements made by the United Nations. Quite rightly so. These pacts guarantee something the United Nations cannot—that action can be taken if the Soviet Union or a country associated with it attempts to commit aggression against any of the signatory powers. There is no real contradiction between regional security pacts and the peace-keeping functions of the United Nations so long as the pacts do not crystallize into blocks, each dominated by a great power, within the U.N.

The U.N. in Action

The Charter prohibition against the use of force as an instrument of national policy has not been well honored. Many large-scale conflicts have been resolved outside the U.N. but in some disputes the United Nations has been able to halt the fighting and to prevent the spread of the conflict. An examination of the peace-keeping record shows that the U.N. can on occasion be a useful instrument when the members wish to use it. It has not been able to resolve the political differences which created the conflict in the first instance, but it was never empowered to do so.

One of the early disputes in which the United Nations became involved was the India-Pakistan disagreement over Kashmir. The argument arose when the Hindu ruler would not allow his state to join a Moslem nation—Pakistan—even though the majority of his people were Moslems. Pakistan used Kashmir tribesmen to initiate hostilities, and the Hindu ruler of Kashmir asked India for protection. Thus, Indian troops occupied about two-thirds of Kashmir during 1946 and fought Pakistani troops who occupied the remainder. India accused Pakistan of aggression in January 1948 before the Security Council. The Council responded by sending a fact-finding and mediation commission to the area. It recommended a cease-fire, a truce, and a plebiscite. The cease-fire went into effect in January 1949, but there has been no truce or plebiscite. India refuses to allow a vote because she insists that Pakistan, as an aggressor, should not be allowed to benefit from it. The real reason may be fear of being outvoted. Pakistan asked the

---

[13] Geoffrey L. Goodwin, *Britain and the United Nations* (New York: Manhattan Publishing Co., 1957), pp. 9-10.

Security Council to call for a withdrawal of all troops but the resolution was not adopted. And here the issue remains, with the U.N. still keeping its eye on the cease-fire. Although the U.N. succeeded in stopping the fighting, it has been unable to make any progress in the political settlement which must be made before peace really returns to the area.

An entirely different type of U.N. action was called for by the North Korean attack on South Korea in June of 1950. The problem of the unification of Korea on the basis of free elections had been turned over to the U.N. by the U.S. in 1947. The divided country was, then, a matter of U.N. concern *prior* to the invasion. The attack could be viewed as a deliberate effort to thwart the peaceful unification of Korea by the U.N.; the North Koreans intended to present the world with a *fait accompli*. Thanks to the absence of the Soviet Union, the Security Council, in a series of resolutions, took the opportunity to recognize that North Korea had committed a breach of the peace, to call for withdrawal of her forces, and to request U.N. members for assistance "to repel the armed attack and to restore international peace and security in the area." It should be obvious that the U.N. action in 1950 was not of the type originally expected—peace-keeping by all the great powers—but rather a recommendation that members contribute military forces to be used on an *ad hoc* basis. It was a significant contribution to international peace because "this first use of collective measures against a breach of the peace amounted to a major diplomatic breakthrough in the attempt to discourage open aggression." [14] The United States and South Korea carried the major burden of the conduct of the war, but 15 other members did send military aid, and 45 made some contribution to the effort. Many neutralist countries would not contribute and some deplored the " 'use' of the U.N. in the service of American national interests." [15] These critics ignored, of course, the U.N.'s involvement with Korea prior to June of 1950.

The U.N. was called upon to make additional decisions regarding Korea as a result of the large-scale intervention by Communist China in late 1950. Before the intervention, however, the General Assembly had adopted a resolution favoring a united democratic Korea and had established a U.N. Commission for the Unification and Rehabilitation of Korea. This action broadened the U.N.'s participation in Korea beyond the mere checking of the aggressor as first approved in the summer of 1950. The intervention of the Communist Chinese again presented the U.N. with a deliberate flouting of its authority and influence. Because of the Uniting for Peace Resolution,

---

[14] Fred Greene, *Dynamics of International Relations* (New York: Holt, Rinehart and Winston, 1964), p. 535.

[15] *Ibid.*, p. 536.

which had been approved on November 2, 1950, the General Assembly was able to assert the voice of the majority when the Security Council became deadlocked. On February 1, 1951, the General Assembly approved a resolution which condemned Communist China as an aggressor and imposed an arms embargo. No sanctions were imposed—even though they could have been under the Charter—because many members believed such an action would only result in an expansion of the conflict, perhaps even into a global war. The U.N. assumed a key role, therefore, in limiting military action by its executive agent, the U.S. The truce of 1953 stopped the fighting and returned Korea to the approximate *status quo ante;* the U.N. has since been frustrated by the North Koreans in its efforts to carry out its resolutions to unify Korea by peaceful means.

The Suez crisis of 1956 presented the United Nations with a dispute unlike Kashmir or Korea. In this instance two of the permanent members of the Security Council were charged with having committed aggression. Britain and France believed their vital national interests were threatened when Egypt nationalized the Suez Canal, but they waited for the Security Council to find a solution to this complicated and inflammatory problem. The situation changed when Israel launched a preventive war against Egypt. Britain and France issued an ultimatum and followed it with an invasion aimed at securing their treaty rights in the canal area. The Security Council was unable to issue an order to force an Israeli withdrawal because of a French and British veto, and the matter passed to the General Assembly under the Uniting for Peace Resolution. An American-sponsored resolution calling for a cease-fire and the withdrawal of forces was passed by the General Assembly on November 2, 1956. At this point a significant contribution to international organization was made by Canada when it urged the adoption of a resolution empowering the Secretary-General to prepare a plan for a United Nations Emergency Force. This effort succeeded primarily because Britain and France agreed to stop fighting if the U.N. force would keep the peace between Israel and Egypt. Egypt agreed to the entry of U.N. troops on its soil, and British and French forces were withdrawn. Israel refused to evacuate the Sinai Peninsula until March 1957, and it has never allowed UNEF units on its soil. To this date, a U.N. force remains on patrol on the Egyptian side of the Israeli border.

Another type of peace-keeping role was played by the United Nations in Laos. In 1958 the Government of Laos protested to the Security Council that Communist North Vietnam was supporting Laotian guerrillas inside Laos. The Council approved the dispatch of a fact-finding group to the area, a proposal made possible because the Council President ruled the item was of a procedural nature and thus not subject to a Soviet veto. The U.N. group reported to the Council that the Laotian charges were unfounded. This was not the end of the story. Late in 1959 the Secretary-General, Dag Hammarskjold, went to Laos, without authorization from the General Assembly or the Security Council, when major hostilities broke out between the Communist and government forces in the country. Hammarskjold hoped he could help keep the peace and re-establish a coalition government. Upon his departure from Laos he left behind a permanent U.N. representative "whose presence, he hoped, would help keep the peace and restore a moderate coalition government." [16] This hope proved abortive, and only the conclusion of an American-Russian agreement—with the U.N. not involved—restored temporary peace to the area.

The 1960 Congo crisis posed new major peace-keeping problems for the U.N. Belgium suddenly gave the Congo its freedom in July 1960, and the resultant confusion and lack of established authority led to the collapse of public discipline and open conflict between two rival authorities for control of the government. Belgian military forces which were still in the Congo were used to protect the white inhabitants, and the Government of the Congo asked for U.N. assistance to halt "Belgian aggression." The Secretary-General took the initiative and called a meeting of the Security Council. A resolution sponsored by Tunisia calling for the dispatch of a U.N. force to the area was passed, and its implementation left largely in the hands of Mr. Hammarskjold. A force was quickly assembled which did not contain any elements from the large powers. The Secretary-General was principally concerned with the restoration of internal order as soon as possible in order to avoid any great-power intervention in the dispute. The situation deteriorated when the Katanga region refused entry to the U.N. forces, and the U.N. refused to fight its way in. The Security Council requested the immediate withdrawal of Belgian troops, and this was accomplished as a U.N. force of 15,000 to 20,000—composed mostly of African contingents—entered the Congo.

Internal political developments made the job of the U.N. more difficult when Patrice Lumumba, then head of the Congo Government, made arrangements to receive Soviet aid. A coup unseated Lumumba, and his Soviet advisers were ousted from the country. Each major political and military development in the Congo was followed by increased U.N. involvement in the crisis, eventually going far beyond the initial intention of restoring law and order to include the maintenance of public services and assistance to the government in fulfilling its administrative tasks. The Secretary-General's job

---

[16] *Ibid.*, p. 571.

was made more difficult because of the vacillations of the contributing powers, many of which took sides with the contending Congolese factions. The major factor which held the operation together was Hammarskjold's repeated warnings that unless the U.N. handled this problem satisfactorily, the Congo, and thus Africa, would be turned into a major center of struggle in the cold war.

The Security Council finally approved a resolution which empowered the Secretary-General not only to clear the Congo of the foreign mercenaries in the pay of the secessionists but also to end the disorder by fighting back if necessary. This stronger U.N. action was made possible because of Lumumba's murder, which brought home to the more timid members of the U.N. the necessity for strong decisive action. U.N. forces moved into Katanga and some fighting ensued between the local forces and the U.N. contingent. It was during an attempt to investigate the Katanga situation that Dag Hammarskjold was killed in an airplane crash. The Acting Secretary-General, U Thant, was given even greater power to resolve the problem and restore order when he was authorized to use force not just in self-defense or to prevent civil war but to maintain the territorial integrity and independence of the Congo and to help its government restore law and order. It was not until January 1963, that the threat of Katanga secession was dissipated as a result of U.N. military action against the rebel strongholds. Although peace was temporarily restored to the Congo, the larger political question of factionalism was not resolved. Nor was the role the membership expects the U.N. to play in the continuing struggle. The Congo operations were a great strain on the organization. It ran short of funds; it did not enjoy the political support of France, Britain, and Belgium; and the smaller powers lost a golden opportunity to use the U.N. as an effective peace-keeping instrument. The Secretary-General was directed to accomplish virtual miracles but was not given the firm support he required from the members. The operations in the Congo point up the lack of agreement in the world community on the direction the U.N. is supposed to take in crises of this nature.

The efforts of the U.N. to keep the peace are more impressive than those of the League of Nations, but it is hard to say where they are leading. The most significant action taken under U.N. auspices, the Korean conflict, is not likely to happen again in the same way. It may have been the last time that U.S. troops would be used in a U.N. police action to meet a direct challenge by a Communist power to the U.N. authority. The part played by the U.N. in the Suez, Laos, and Congo crises placed great strains on the institution itself. It could be justified only on the grounds that a dispute which might involve great power intervention and thus turn the area into a major battlefield was of concern to the U.N. even if it called for interference to preserve internal law and order. The military forces that were put at U.N. disposal in these and other crises, such as Cyprus, came from the middle and smaller powers, not from the great powers, which were supposed to keep the peace. But even this approach will meet with rough going. The Soviet Union, for example, is unwilling to pay a share of the Congo expenses because it does not want the Secretary-General to be able to intervene in the domestic affairs of weaker states if intervention does not suit Soviet interest. Now that the General Assembly has more influence than formerly and is overflowing with new states, the Soviet position on the financial issue may have a very real appeal to the big powers. The adjournment of the General Assembly in February 1965 was ostensibly due to a wish to avoid applying Article 19, but the real reason, which lay behind the financial one, was a difference of views over the role of the Secretariat, over which issue there is plenty of room for disagreement.

The main lesson to be drawn from these U.N. peace-keeping actions is that it may not be wise to bring the U.N. into every dispute that may lead to war. The problem for the U.S. is to distinguish between those cases that can be handled by the U.N., under existing arrangements, to the advantage of the U.S. and its allies, and those which should be dealt with by other means, for example, Vietnam. Even if the distinction is made correctly, no easy task, the problem of securing the cooperation of the U.N. may be even more difficult.

III.

THE PROBLEMS OF MEMBERSHIP

The Expansion of the General Assembly

The General Assembly was conceived as the most democratic element in the United Nations structure. Here no veto prevails, and each member state has but one vote. This was intended to be, and has largely proved to be, the forum of the world. It is not a legislative body, it cannot enact binding laws, it can only pass resolutions and appeal to world public opinion. It is one of the organs through which agreement can be achieved.

The General Assembly is the only organ of the United Nations in which all members are represented. Its growth in size—membership has more than doubled—has drawn attention to the conduct of its operations. The General Assembly allows the smallest member to have as much of a voice as the largest. Nor is there any reluctance on the part of the new representatives to speak on issues before the Assembly both loudly and frequently and at great length. Regardless of the issue, all members have the "sovereign" right to present a point of view, and there are no rules of cloture.

The sheer size of the Assembly has increased the difficulties in its work, especially in view of the shortness of its sessions.

. . . The United States (along with the membership as a whole) tends to regard the General Assembly as a three-months spectacle which folds its tents at season's end and goes into winter quarters. The quantity,

33

range and complexity of the agenda of the General Assembly require that the diplomatic show be kept on the road all year around.[1]

The keeping of the peace is a full-time job. It is in the "riotous and scandalous sessions" of the General Assembly, as General de Gaulle has called them, that the world has been treated to the unruly, certainly the unparliamentary, behavior of Mr. Khrushchev, to bitter and acrimonious name-calling, to walk-outs, and to gallery disturbances from nationalist groups. Such phenomena were put into proper perspective by Trygve Lie when he said, "I would rather hear the worst insults of an angry debate in the General Assembly of the United Nations than read the exquisitely polite and dignified language in which foreign offices know how to couch a declaration of war."[2]

The General Assembly has increased both in size and importance. It is in the General Assembly that the United Nations has felt the impact of the newer members, members who are not primarily concerned with the peace-keeping functions of the organization. Many of these new members are creations of the United Nations, or their independence was inspired in some manner by the United Nations, if only by fostering a climate in which the retention of colonies became more and more difficult. Many of the new nations tend to look to the United Nations to solve their own internal domestic problems, matters explicitly excluded from U.N. action by the Charter. These underdeveloped and largely uncommitted nations have the majority vote in the General Assembly, a fact that could lead to major changes in the policies adopted by the United Nations. As Mr. Joseph E. Johnson, former adviser to the State Department on United Nations affairs, has pointed out:

> If the present and foreseeable membership and activities of the United Nations tell us anything, it is that the central concerns of that organization will reflect increasingly the central concerns of the new states. And the concerns of the new states do not involve, as a matter of primary interest, the achievement of international order and stability. They involve, rather, the substantiation of national independence and the assertion of the international power to which the new states feel entitled by virtue of their numbers.[3]

---

[1] Gross, *op. cit.*, p. 74.

[2] Quoted in *United Nations—Its Records and its Prospects, op. cit.*, p. 24.

[3] Joseph E. Johnson, "Helping to Build New States," in Francis O. Wilcox and H. Field Haviland, Jr., *The United States and The United Nations* (Baltimore: Johns Hopkins Press, 1961), p. 3.

The increased role of the General Assembly came about through American initiative. At the San Francisco conference the small nations had pressed for a revision of the Dumbarton Oaks proposals in order to give the General Assembly greater jurisdiction and authority than had been originally planned. The big powers did not favor expanding the role of this body. But owing largely to Australia's efforts the General Assembly, in Article 10, was empowered to discuss any question or matter "within the scope of the present Charter or relating to the powers and functions of any organs provided for in the present Charter." [4] It was this highly important amendment that made it possible for the United States to propose the adoption in November 1950 of the Uniting for Peace Resolution in which the General Assembly asserted its right to meet in emergency session when there is a threat to the peace and the Security Council has been unable to agree upon a course of action. The occasion was the return of the Soviet Union to the Security Council in August 1950 after an absence of seven months, thus making the Security Council useless as an instrument for furthering the goals of the United Nations in Korea. One of the first actions of the Assembly after the Uniting for Peace Resolution, the condemnation of Communist China as an aggressor in Korea (January 1951), clearly indicated the potentialities of the Assembly. As Dag Hammarskjold put it: "It is not the Soviet Union, or indeed any other big powers, who need the U.N. for their protection, it is all the others. In this sense the Organization is first of all *their* organization. . . ." [5]

The Soviet Union, Great Britain, and France have charged that the principles of the Charter were violated in the Uniting for Peace Resolution because it relieves the Big Five of their Charter responsibilities for maintaining peace. They advocate a return to the Charter. They point out that the Charter was not intended to be used by member states, large or small, as a vehicle to settle internal, national problems or to pursue national objectives which have little or no direct bearing on the maintenance of peace by collective security. The new nations tend to be less interested in the first mission of the U.N., the maintenance of peace and security, than in the second mission, the achievement of international cooperation on worldwide problems in the economic, social, cultural, and humanitarian fields. It is because the great powers fear that the new nations, if they can increase the power of the General Assembly to take action, may have too much influence on the peace-keeping function that they are alarmed at these developments and talk about returning to the Charter.

---

[4] Evatt, *op. cit.*, pp. 19-20.
[5] Quoted in Boyd, *United Nations: Piety, Myth and Truth, op. cit.*, p. 178.

36

Their fear has some validity. Mr. Eichelberger, for example, expresses the views of many when he says,

It is inevitable that the General Assembly, growing as the United Nations approaches universality, will be the parliament of nations. It will be the place where the hopes and the protests of the nations can be expressed. As it approaches universality, it will be the spokesman for over one hundred nations in attendance. It can become a mighty moral and legal force. It will outstrip any other body. If the past is any indication, it will become a legislative body.[6]

In his recent book, *The Four Faces of Peace,* Lester B. Pearson writes:

Tennyson's parliament of man is a vision for which many men have worked, and not a few have died, to bring to reality in the United Nations. We may still fail to achieve this vision; but we may not. In any case, we have no right to abandon the dream because it has not yet been realized in the United Nation's glass palace on Manhattan.[7]

The United States Government is also aware that if the new nations come to have a decisive influence in the Assembly and the Assembly asserts a major role in United Nations affairs, many of the decisions may very well not fit in with the national interest of the United States.

The uncommitted, newly-emerged Afro-Asian nations have an absolute majority in the Assembly and can thus control all procedural matters. Control of over one-third of the votes also gives them the power to block Assembly action on important (substantive) questions. It is the power of the new nations to affect such issues that disturbs the United States Government, not because the Assembly's decisions are binding but because the Assembly may cease to be a useful instrument for keeping the peace. Senator Henry Jackson of Washington had this matter very much in mind when he criticized the United States' position on the United Nations as follows:

The United Nations is, and shall continue to be, an important avenue of American foreign policy. Yet practices have developed which, I believe, lead to an undue influence of U.N. considerations in our national decision-making. Indeed it is necessary to ask whether the involvement of the U.N. in our policy-making has not at times hampered the wise definition of our national interests and the development of sound policies for their advancement.[8]

---

[6] Eichelberger, *op. cit.,* p. 115.
[7] Pearson, *op. cit.,* p. 92.
[8] Quoted in Moore, *op. cit.,* p. 47.

In this connection, it may be well to clarify the question of bloc voting, a subject that has taken on new life since the so-called Afro-Asian bloc has increased its numbers in the U.N. It is not unnatural for members of any political organization to group themselves together in blocs. What is important is the degree to which the blocs are temporary or permanent, free and shifting associations or disciplined units. Except for Molotov, who assumed that the United States would have complete control over the votes of the Latin American countries, no one at San Francisco anticipated the problem because no one anticipated the vast increase in U.N. membership, the changing role of the General Assembly, or the impact of the cold war. If we define a bloc as "a group of states which meets regularly in caucus and the members of which are bound in their votes in the General Assembly by the caucus decision," [9] then there has been only one bloc in the U.N.— the Soviet bloc. There are other groups that meet more or less regularly but do not bind themselves to vote in any given way, and many other shifting groupings, the most consistent of which have a regional basis.

The United States has usually been able to secure approval of its proposals in the U.N. or to prevent action by others inimical to U.S. interests. The two U.S. congressional members of the U.S. delegation to the Eighteenth General Assembly noted in their report that although the U.S. and its allies no longer commanded an automatic majority in the General Assembly, the "record of the Eighteenth session shows a definite absence of any developments injurious to the vital interests of our country and of the other Western powers." [10] On the other hand, the new situation in the Assembly will undoubtedly call for much more strenuous efforts on the part of the U.S. delegation than it has had to exercise in the past in order to command a majority in favor of U.S. policies. In his study, *Bloc Politics in the United Nations,* Thomas Hovet claims that the United States has not done a good job in maintaining contact with the informal groupings in the U.N., and that the time has come for the exercise of quiet diplomatic techniques rather than crisis diplomacy and diplomatic arm-twisting. According to Hovet,

> The United States commands a majority only by political and economic pressure and not by developing trust and understanding. Past successes are not necessarily a clue to future ones . . . bloc politics in the General Assembly can no longer be viewed as a temporary phenomenon. Blocs and groups now constitute a regularized, though informal, aspect of

[9] Thomas Hovet, *Bloc Politics in the United Nations* (Cambridge, Mass.: Harvard University Press, 1960), p. 119.

[10] *United Nations in Crisis,* Union Calendar No. 457, House Report No. 1103, 88th Congress, 2d Session, January 28, 1964, p. 1.

38

the Organization of the United Nations; and there is every reason to believe that with the present voting arrangements they will play an increasing role.[11]

Hovet may be right about the future of the blocs but is over-critical of the U.S. delegation's efforts to keep contact with other delegates. However, the new nations create very real problems which have to be handled in such a way as not to discourage their participation in the U.N. Organization and the world community.

It is inevitable that the new countries should see the United Nations as a testing ground of the sincerity of the former colonial powers and should therefore be oversensitive about their treatment, especially on anything resembling what they would think of as colonialism. Mr. Joseph E. Johnson has related this whole problem to their specific concern for their own national unification:

> We of the older states must realize that the problem of unification is something different from economic and social development and different from establishing "law and order." If we fail to understand this, and if the United Nations do not reflect that understanding, the new states may well be tempted to acquiesce in the destruction of the Organization itself. This is one of the great lessons of the Congo experience. Many of us failed to realize that the African states could not admit the possibility of Katangan secession, could not even support United Nations negotiations with Katanga as a quasi-independent state; to have done so would have been to have encouraged by implication every divisive tendency in their own countries.[12]

The problem is how to give these new nations a real sense of participation and responsibility in world affairs, particularly the preservation of peace, and satisfy their hopes and plans for modernization, also a major concern of the United Nations, without giving them a political influence in the United Nations out of all proportion to their real strength and political maturity.

Universal or Selective Membership?

The sponsors of the United Nations did not want or provide for universality of membership in 1945. Membership in the United Nations has always been conditional. The initial membership was limited to those powers which had signed the Washington declaration of January 1, 1942, a statement in the common cause against the Axis powers. All enemy countries were

---

[11] Hovet, op. cit., p. 119.
[12] Johnson, op. cit., pp. 12-13.

excluded, as were those countries which had not openly opposed the Axis powers. Fifty-one nations signed the Charter qualifying as original members. But while limiting the initial membership, the founders provided for the admission of new members. It can be argued that Article 4 of the Charter is designed to provide for eventual but conditional universality:

1. Membership in the United Nations is open to all other peace-loving states which accept the obligations contained in the present Charter and, in the judgment of the Organization, are able and willing to carry out these obligations.

2. The admission of any such state to membership in the United Nations will be effected by a decision of the General Assembly upon the recommendation of the Security Council.

There have been many bitter battles in the Security Council over the admission of new members, including disputes as to whether or not the veto should apply to membership applications. The International Court of Justice rendered an advisory opinion on whether other conditions for membership could be imposed besides those stated in the Charter. It decided in the negative. No new conditions, in other words, could be imposed. This disposed of the original Soviet position that it could not vote for the admission of a new member with which it did not have diplomatic relations. The Soviets used the veto virtually to freeze U.N. membership until 1955, at which time the U.S. agreed to a series of package deals—the U.S. accepting Soviet-sponsored states in return for Soviet acceptance of U.S. candidates —and many new members joined the Organization. The rapid admission of the newly-formed states in the early 1960's seemed to create the impression that any new state could expect early admission to membership.

The trend toward universality of membership as far as the new Afro-Asian nations were concerned was in sharp contrast to the refusal to agree on membership for Germany, Korea, and Vietnam. All these states have in common the fact that they are divided areas with competing anti-Communist and Communist governments contending for *the* seat in the United Nations. Because it is one of the Big Five, China has always been the most controversial case of all. There is no question of admitting China to the United Nations; China is already a member and was one of the sponsoring powers. The real question is which government, the Communist or the Nationalist, shall represent China. The answer to this question was postponed by every General Assembly session until 1961, when the U.S. agreed to an Assembly vote on the specific question of Chinese representation and the Assembly voted to reject Peiping's claims.[13]   There is no question but that this explosive and complex problem will be all the more difficult to handle now that Peiping has become a nuclear power.

The China Issue

The problem of Chinese representation in the United Nations should not be confused with the problem of deciding whether or not the U.S. should recognize the Peiping regime.   Representation and recognition are separate problems; one does not necessarily follow from the other.   Many of the members of the United Nations do not have diplomatic relations with each other; for example, Cuba and Outer Mongolia do not have diplomatic relations with the United States.   The corridors of the United Nations building serve as a meeting place for representatives of countries which have no diplomatic relations, just as they are used by small nations that cannot afford to maintain embassies all over the world for the purposes of conventional diplomacy.   As the International Court of Justice ruled, recognition and admission are separate problems and have no bearing on each other.

The trend toward universality of membership in the United Nations, with the consequent lowering of the standards for admission, naturally weakens the stand of the United States against Chinese Communist representation. While there is little doubt that Communist China, in view of her attack on the U.N. in Korea and her unwillingness to observe agreements she freely signed, does not qualify for representation under the Provisions of Article 4, many of the nations admitted since 1945 have also not qualified under this article because the package deals have "eroded" the conditions for admission laid out in the Charter.   In the words of Ernest Gross:

> In view of the character of certain of these states, such as Albania, Hungary, Rumania, and Bulgaria, the Organization ignored Article 4 and expressed no judgment as to their ability, or willingness, to carry out their obligations.   The Assembly resolution limited itself to noting a "general feeling in favor of the universality of the United Nations. . . ."[14]

Soviet use of the veto to freeze membership until we accepted the package deal was probably done with deliberate calculation in order to undermine the moral and political basis of selection.   Struggle over the selection of new members was an important front of the cold war.

The General Assembly has made two basic decisions regarding the China

---

[13] See Appendix C for 1950-63 voting record of the General Assembly on Chinese representation.

[14] Gross, *op. cit.*, pp. 63-64.

representation question. The first one, made in 1950, recommended that when a conflict over representation existed, "the attitude adopted by the General Assembly . . . should be taken into account in other organs of the United Nations and in the specialized agencies." [15] Simply stated, this meant that if the General Assembly accepted the Communist regime as the representative of China, the other organs of the United Nations such as the Security Council and the specialized agencies would be expected to follow suit. There is no precedent, however, for this situation. No one is certain whether it is technically possible to admit Communist China to the General Assembly while the Government of the Republic of China remains in the Security Council. It is certainly politically unlikely that this could happen, as Peiping has made it clear that it is not interested in representation unless the National Government is completely removed from all organs of the U.N. Article 23 of the Charter merely lists the five permanent members of the Security Council. The veto does not apply to the selection of non-permanent members by the General Assembly. Under Article 27, procedural matters are not subject to the veto while decisions "on all other matters" must have the affirmative votes of all the permanent members. Whether the Chinese representation question on the Security Council is procedural or "other" has never been decided by the Security Council, which is where it has to be decided. It was not clear in the General Assembly whether the representation issue would be decided by a straight majority or a two-thirds vote until December 1961, when the Sixteenth Session adopted a resolution to the effect that representation is an "important question." [16] Article 18 of the U.N. Charter provides that decisions of the General Assembly on important questions shall be made by a two-thirds majority of the members present and voting. This means that one-third of the members of the U.N. can prevent the seating of the Peiping regime as the representative of China so long as the General Assembly continues to treat it as an "important question." Of equal importance is the fact that these two resolutions effectively transfer the China representation question from the Security Council to the General Assembly.

What of the attitude of Communist China? Peiping has always taken steps to keep the record clear that there is only one China and that Peiping has an indisputable claim to the Chinese seat in the Security Council and all other U.N. organs. The Communist regime has consistently opposed

[15] Quoted in H. Arthur Steiner, "Communist China in The World Community," *International Conciliation,* May 1961, pp. 446-47.

[16] United Nations General Assembly, Sixteenth Session, Official Records, 1080th Plenary Meeting, Friday, December 15, 1961.

the whole concept of two Chinas. As early as 1945, Mao Tse-tung stated that the Chinese Communist Party approved of the Dumbarton Oaks Conference proposals and welcomed the San Francisco conference of United Nations representatives.[17] It is not always recalled that Tung Pi-wu, a well-known member of the Chinese Communist Party, was in the Chinese delegation in San Francisco. In 1950 the Foreign Minister, Chou En-lai, designated Peiping's representatives to the United Nations and called for the removal of the "illegitimate delegates of the Chinese Kuomintang reactionary clique."[18] In this same year the United Nations Secretary-General, Trygve Lie, tried to work out a solution to the problem in a famous memorandum (Security Council document S/1466), in which he argued that recognition and representation were two different and separate problems. He claimed that the point at issue, in case of dispute, was a purely factual one— who actually ruled the people and the territory concerned.

Rejection of Trygve Lie's proposals, which would have led directly to the acceptance of the Chinese Communist representatives, provoked the withdrawal of the Soviet Union from the Security Council from January to August 1950. At this time the United States had apparently written off the Nationalist Government but was not ready to accept immediately the claims of the Chinese Communists. We were waiting for the dust to settle. The Korean War and subsequent Chinese intervention resolved this problem for the United States. As a further consequence of the Korean War, the claim of the Chinese People's Republic has been prejudiced by the General Assembly Resolution of February 1951 which labeled Peiping an aggressor in Korea and by Peiping's subsequent refusal to accept U.N. post-truce proposals for political unification of Korea. It is entirely consistent with Peiping's views of the world situation that it should consider its determination to recover Taiwan by force, if necessary, a matter outside the jurisdiction of the U.N. This view was supported by the Soviet Union in the United Nations in 1961 when its representatives said, "The government of the People's Republic of China has the right to liquidate the clique of Chiang Kai-shek, both by peaceful means and by the use of force; that is within its exclusive right and nobody else's."[19]

The same assumptions hold in regard to Tibet. The General Assembly resolution condemning the suppression of the Tibetan revolt in 1959 was denounced by Chinese writers as being in violation of Article 2 (7), which

---

[17] *The Selected Works of Mao Tse-tung* (Peking, 1953), Vol. III, p. 1108.
[18] Quoted in Steiner, "Communist China in the World Community," *op. cit.*, p. 443.
[19] *Department of State Bulletin,* November 19, 1962, p. 789.

excludes matters within the domestic jurisdiction of any state from the jurisdiction of the U.N. On this point, the Nationalist Government would agree with Peiping, as indeed it does on the question of Taiwan. Both the Communists and the Nationalists consider Taiwan to be a province of China, and both believe there can be only one China. Nor would Chiang Kai-shek willingly give up the use of force to recover the mainland.

It may be an open question whether or not Communist China gives representation in the U.N. a high priority in its foreign policy goals, but it is certain that Peiping has paid a great deal of attention to the U.N. Organization and has usually made its position clear on all important actions of that body. It is not surprising that the People's Republic of China, which expects eventually to represent China in the Security Council, usually resists all changes in the Charter. Nor is it surprising that Peiping has approved some of the peace-keeping efforts of the U.N. and disapproved of others. She has approved only those actions that appear to damage the interests of the Western powers. Peiping supported Egypt's claims to sole control over the Suez Canal and approved the efforts of the U.N. to get the United States out of Lebanon in 1958. On some occasions Peiping has criticized resolutions of the United Nations on various grounds, one of the most interesting of which is the population argument. Chinese commentators estimate how the total population of the states voting on one side of a resolution compares with the total population on the other side. For example, the U.N. General Assembly resolution of October 7, 1950, permitting the U.N. command in Korea to go beyond the 38th parallel, was denounced on the grounds that it was not supported by a majority of the population represented in the United Nations. Perhaps the best summary of Peiping's attitude toward the international community can be taken from a report of the National People's Congress Standing Committee in January 1960: "China will unhesitatingly commit itself to international obligations to which it agrees"— and only when it has been consulted.

The United States' opposition to the claims of the People's Republic was stated quite adequately by President Eisenhower in his last State of the Union Message of January 1961, when he said: "This country has continued to withhold recognition of Communist China and to oppose vigorously the admission of this belligerent and unrepentant nation into the United Nations. Red China has yet to demonstrate that it deserves to be considered a peace-loving nation." The same theme was advanced by Adlai Stevenson before the U.N. General Assembly on October 16, 1963, when he said: "The government in Peiping is not peace-loving; it does not concur in the obligations which the Charter imposes and it is clearly neither able nor willing to carry them out." [20]

The Congress of the United States has expressed itself very clearly on the question of Chinese representation. In July 1953, the House Committee on Foreign Affairs drafted a resolution which expressed the sense of the Congress: "That the Chinese Communists are not entitled to and should not be recognized to represent China in the United Nations." [21] This resolution did not pass the Congress because of the pressure for adjournment, but the Congress felt so strongly on the Chinese representation issue that in the year 1961 it took three specific actions in relation to Communist China. The first of these was the Senate concurrent resolution No. 34 of August 31, 1961. This document states the position of the United States Government at that time so clearly that it is worth recalling the main points. The resolution reaffirmed our treaty obligations with the Government of the Republic of China, and noted that the government had discharged its obligations under the Charter of the United Nations. On the other hand, it denounced the Chinese Communist Government for flagrant violations of basic human rights, for imposing on the Chinese people one of the most brutal regimes known to history, and charged that it was without authority to speak for the Chinese people other than the authority derived from usurpation and tyranny. The resolution recalled the Chinese Communist aggression in Korea, repression in Tibet, failure to release American prisoners as promised, and its export of narcotics to non-Communist countries on a massive scale (the United Nations has been very active in trying to suppress the international illicit narcotics traffic), and its general hostility to the United Nations. The Congress therefore resolved to continue its opposition to the seating of the Chinese Communist regime in the United Nations, and to support the President in not according diplomatic recognition. [22]

The second action taken by the Congress was the adoption of an amendment to the Department of State Appropriation Act: "It is the sense of the Congress that the Communist Chinese government should not be admitted to membership in the United Nations as the representative of China." [23] The third action taken by the Congress was a statement included in the

---

[20] *Department of State Bulletin,* November 11, 1963, p. 755.

[21] *Review of the United Nations Charter,* 83d Congress, 2d Session, Document No. 87, Subcommittee on the United Nations Charter, January 7, 1954, pp. 178-82.

[22] Senate Concurrent Resolution 34, *United States Statutes at Large,* 1961, Vol. 75, pp. 965-66. See Appendix D, for full text of this resolution.

[23] Public Law 87-267, September 21, 1961, *United States Statutes at Large,* Vol. 75, p. 550.

Foreign Assistance and Related Agencies Appropriation Act. Of particular significance in Section 107 is the following statement:

> In the event of the seating of representatives of the Chinese Communist regime in the Security Council or General Assembly of the United Nations, the President is requested to inform the Congress insofar as is compatible with the requirements of national security, of the implications of this action upon the foreign policy of the United States and our foreign relationships, including that created by membership in the United Nations, together with any recommendations which he may have with respect to the matter.[24]

There is every reason to expect that the attitude of Congress reflects that of the majority of the American people and that no switch in attitude or policy can be expected. As the Senate resolution points out, the United States has close treaty relations with the Government of the Republic of China and these are clearly related to United States interests in the Western Pacific.

The China representation issue goes to the heart of the problem of membership and therefore of the character and purposes of the U.N. In spite of the clear position of the Senate, it disturbs American public and professional opinion. There are many who would agree with the following statement of the problem:

> The basic anomaly, then, is the vital role China plays in the life of the international community and in the future of its members, in spite of the non-participation of the People's Republic in general international organizations and the aura of reciprocal hostility that surrounds CPR relations with so many other states. China cannot be exorcised by magic charms and incantations, and others cannot settle its fate for it. The China problem has become the prime problem of the entire world community, *China included,* and statesmanship of the order required to produce a tolerable solution has yet to make its appearance.[25]

The anomaly is not the vitality but the character of the role that Peiping plays. It is true, as is so often ponderously proclaimed, that Peiping cannot be wished out of existence, but this does not necessarily demand formal recognition. The U.S. has had over 130 meetings, on the ambassadorial level, with the Communist regime (in Warsaw and Geneva), whereas

---

[24] Public Law 87-329, September 30, 1961, *United States Statutes at Large,* Vol. 75, pp. 718-19.

[25] Steiner, *op. cit.,* p. 393.

the British chargé d'affaires in Peiping has no contact with the Foreign Minister, only his subordinates.   At the present time the U.S. takes the position that the admission of Peiping to the U.N. would further neither of two considerations highly relevant to U.S. policy—the healthy development of the United Nations and the ending of the cold war.

IV.

THE PROBLEM OF MILITARY POWER

Whatever might have been, the arms race has in fact proceeded at a fantastic pace. There is no doubt whatsoever that the greatest quantitative and qualitative growth in armaments that has ever taken place in the history of the world has coincided with the first two decades of the existence of the United Nations. In 1945 there was only one country in the world that had nuclear capacity; today there are five, and the number is bound to increase. The present situation was described by President Johnson in January 1964 in a letter to a U.N.-sponsored Eighteen-Nation Committee on disarmament at Geneva:

> In a matter of moments you can wipe out from 50 to 100 million of our adversaries or they can, in the same amount of time, wipe out 50 to 100 million of our people, taking half of our land, half our population, in the matter of an hour. So general war is impossible and some alternatives are essential.[1]

These basic facts have produced a greater sense of urgency than the world has ever known before for the control and regulation, if not for the elimination, of the enormous powers of destruction now at our command.

The framers of the Charter were keenly aware of the relationship between collective security and disarmament. Warned by the experience of the

---

[1] United States Arms Control and Disarmament Agency, Publication 23, July 1964, p. iii.

League, whose interminable conferences on disarmament achieved nothing, they emphasized political agreements rather than technical disarmament arrangements; hence the descending order of emphasis in Article 47 from the maintenance of international peace and security to the regulation of armaments and then to "possible disarmament." If the San Francisco meeting had been held in September 1945 after the beginning of the atomic age, there would have been much more emphasis in the Charter on the obligation of members to control arms. It is not impossible that the Baruch Plan might have been written into the Charter. This plan, suggested a year later, called for the creation of an International Atomic Development Authority, which would have a monopoly on the world's production and control of atomic energy. It is certain that the discussions at San Francisco would have been of an entirely different calibre, for the small countries would have pushed strongly for something along the lines of the Baruch Plan. But it is still unlikely that the Soviet Union would have accepted it without the threat of force from the United States.

Arms Control and Disarmament

Disarmament has been on the agenda of every meeting of the General Assembly. The proposals introduced to the General Assembly for the solution of the disarmament problem have been many and varied. They include limitations of armaments, phased disarmament, arms control, disarmament by stages. It is not surprising that the nations which put forward the proposals designed them for their own comparative advantage. The futility of discussing disarmament in the General Assembly with its widely varied membership and enormous contrasts in military strength finally led to the establishment of an eighteen-nation disarmament conference which has met for several years in Geneva. The only tangible results of these meetings so far is the test-ban treaty of 1963, the preliminary work on which was done by a subcommittee of three set up by the Eighteen-Nation Committee. These countries were the United States, the United Kingdom, and the U.S.S.R. The final drafting and signing of the treaty was done in Moscow at the invitation of Khrushchev, and not in Geneva or New York, the headquarters of the U.N. It is also possible that the bilateral agreement for a "hot line" between Washington and Moscow, although arranged entirely outside U.N. auspices, may have owed something to the disarmament discussions in Geneva.

The various steps which led to the conclusion of the partial nuclear test-ban treaty can be traced very briefly. Worldwide demands for the cessation of nuclear testing began in 1954 when a Japanese fishing boat was contaminated by radioactive fallout. India was the first nation other than Japan to raise the issue of radiation before the United Nations. The 1955 Bandung conference of Afro-Asian states urged: "Pending the total prohibition of the manufacture of nuclear and thermonuclear weapons, this conference appeals to all the powers concerned to reach agreement to suspend experiments with such weapons." [2] During the Twelfth General Assembly meeting (1957) the Soviet Union introduced a resolution asking the nuclear nations to agree to suspend nuclear testing for two or three years, beginning January 1, 1958. This resolution was later withdrawn by the Soviet Union. Late in March 1958 the Supreme Soviet declared that the Soviet Union would unilaterally discontinue nuclear tests. On August 22, the United States and the United Kingdom announced their readiness to negotiate a test-ban agreement and indicated they would suspend tests for one year, beginning October 31, 1958.

During the fall of 1958, the Soviet Union and the United States were desperately testing before this deadline was reached. Talks began in Geneva between the three principal nuclear powers on October 31, but the Soviet Union continued to test until November 4, at which time there began a tacit moratorium on testing which lasted until Sepember 1961, when the U.S.S.R. began a series which included explosion of a 50-megaton bomb. In the meantime, France which had never agreed to the moratorium, succeeded in setting off her first nuclear explosion in the Sahara on February 13, 1960.

During most of 1961 the three nuclear powers continued negotiations at Geneva. On September 1, 1961, the Soviet Union resumed nuclear testing. Coincidentally, 25 heads of non-aligned states were meeting in Belgrade at this time. The conference did not condemn the Soviet tests in its communiqué, but many of the heads of states in attendance individually criticized the Soviet resumption of testing.

The United States and the United Kingdom recommended to the Sixteenth General Assembly (1961) that it include on its agenda the following item: "The urgent need for a treaty to ban nuclear weapons tests under effective international control." While the debate was under way on this item, the Soviet Union announced its intention to detonate a 50-megaton explosion. The First Committee of the General Assembly by a vote of 75 to 10 appealed to the Soviet Union to refrain from carrying out this explosion to no avail. The negative votes were all from the Communist bloc.

The Eighteen-Nation Committee on disarmament convened in Geneva on

[2] Homer A. Jack, "Nonalignment and a Test Ban Agreement: The Role of the Non-aligned States," *The Journal of Conflict Resolution,* Proceedings of the International Arms Control Symposium, Ann Arbor, Michigan, December 17-20, 1962, p. 543.

March 14, 1962, and membership in a test-ban subcommittee was confined to the three nuclear powers. However, the eight non-aligned states among the 18 also had an opportunity to participate in debate. The United States also resumed testing, at first underground, in September 1961, and efforts were made by the non-aligned countries to bridge the gap between Russia and the United States. No agreement was reached, and testing continued. By the end of 1962, the United States and the Soviet Union had completed their major series of tests, and the grand total of all devices detonated had reached 433.[3]

The Soviet Union argued during early 1963 that the Geneva conference was bogged down because of Western demands for on-site inspection of Soviet territory, which could not be accepted. Conditions were favorable, in the Soviet view, for the conclusion of a test-ban treaty and it was only prevented "by resistance from the U.S. and its NATO allies." The Soviet attitude was "that when the West starts talking about 'an impasse' and a 'lull' and a sudden 'loss of interest' on the part of the Soviet Union, it is a sure sign that imperialist diplomacy is groping about for arguments and means of frustrating an incipient agreement."[4] Khrushchev argued that Western insistence upon on-site inspection was merely another name for espionage. He reiterated that the Soviet Union was prepared to sign an agreement immediately on the prohibition of all nuclear tests.

The signing of the test-ban treaty in Moscow in August 1963 was hailed as a great achievement for the Communist camp, which cited it as evidence of the "possibility of solving major international problems on mutually acceptable terms if both sides follow the line of peaceful co-existence."[5] The partial test-ban treaty prohibited nuclear testing in outer space, in the atmosphere, and under water; there is no prohibition against underground testing. The treaty, which can be denounced upon three months' notice by any one of the signators, was signed by the sponsoring states—the U.S., U.K., and the U.S.S.R.—and practically every other country in the world except France, Communist China, Israel, and a few other less important countries. The United States and the United Kingdom were willing to agree to this treaty because it is now possible to detect most violations without on-site inspection. The Soviet Union chose to express its hope that the treaty would lead to a settlement of the disarmament issue and to a German

---

[3] *Ibid.,* p. 547.

[4] *International Affairs,* "Strange Lull," No. 7, July 1963 (Moscow), p. 62.

[5] *International Affairs,* "N. S. Khrushchev's Answers to Members of the Association of Newspaper Editors and Publishers of Japan," No. 9, September 1963 (Moscow), p. 4.

peace treaty. Khrushchev warned that "by itself, a nuclear test ban does not yet remove the threat of war, since it does not mean an end to the arms race and even less, disarmament." [6] Soviet editorial writers said the Moscow agreement is the "fruit of the long and stubborn struggles waged by the Soviet Union and the other peace-loving states relying on the support of the peoples of all countries." The Western countries were urged to "show as much statesmanship in other matters as they have done in regard to the test ban, and approach the Soviet peaceable proposals with understanding. [7] Khrushchev's views on the partial test-ban treaty can be summarized under two points. First, the West was forced to conclude the agreement because it had really started the whole nuclear contamination business; and second, Soviet military, scientific, and economic power had erased a Western monopoly of atomic power, hence the correctness of the policy of peaceful coexistence.[8]

The United States has come to see the importance of separating disarmament from arms control. Arms control is the more urgent need and in many ways the approach most likely to produce results. By arms control we mean the regulation of national military power within the existing international system. In other words, arms control relates to measures and agreements, either tacit or overt, that limit or regulate what a nation may do with its existing military power. The nuclear test-ban treaty, for example, belongs to the realm of arms control. It was an open agreement. But there are also tacit agreements, such as the unstated understanding by the Soviet Union and the United States that both will withhold from other nations nuclear technology and weapons. The "hot line" is an arms control measure. So were the moratoriums on testing. So are the measures taken to safeguard us against surprise attack or to prevent accidental war. The twelve-nation treaty of 1959 neutralizing Antarctica, the Austrian state treaty of 1955 neutralizing that country, and the Korean truce arrangements which put a freeze on military forces in North and South Korea and provided for their ultimate withdrawal, are further examples of arms-control measures. Arms control may also include steps taken merely to increase a feeling of mutual confidence as a preliminary for further negotiations. The test-ban treaty is probably the most dramatic instance.

The United States has always considered arms control a necessary first step toward general and complete disarmament. To concentrate upon disarmament alone as the main objective is to court failure. Since 1961 there

---

[6] *Ibid.*
[7] *Ibid.*, "Lessons of The Moscow Talks," p. 70.
[8] *Ibid.*

has been an "official" U.N. definition of disarmament: It is a comprehensive and universal term. It applies to all war-making weapons, nuclear and conventional, and to all types of armed forces and to all nations. General and complete disarmament means the elimination of all national military forces. Each nation would be allowed to keep nothing more in the way of police or militia forces than would be necessary to insure domestic tranquillity. In short, general and complete disarmament calls for the elimination of the war-making capacity of every nation on earth, a visionary goal. As Earl H. Voss puts it in his book *Nuclear Ambush:* "To summarize, the piecemeal approach to disarmament is ineffective; the broad-spectrum approach is physically impossible. Disarmament by conventional means has proved to be what it has been before, a mirage." [9] It is certain that general and complete disarmament is an objective far more difficult to achieve than any plan which aims at arms control, regulation, or limitation.

U.S. and Soviet Positions

The U.S. and Soviet official views as stated at the eighteen-nation disarmament conference are still wide apart. The U.S. view on first-step measures is conveniently summarized in the five-step programs proposed by President Lyndon Johnson on January 22, 1964. The five points were: (1) No nation to use force to solve territorial disputes—either direct or indirect force such as aggression, subversion, or the clandestine supply of arms. (2) The two superpowers and their allies should "agree to explore a verified freeze of the number and characteristics of strategic nuclear offensive and defensive vehicles." This to be accomplished while we continue efforts to achieve general and complete disarmament under effective international control. (3) The U.S. believes that a verified agreement to halt all production of fissionable materials for weapons use would be a major contribution to world peace. The United States would agree to close down its production facilities on a reciprocal plant-by-plant basis. (4) Establishment of a system of worldwide observation posts in order to reduce the danger of accidental, miscalculated or surprise war. (5) The dissemination of nuclear weapons to nations not now controlling them to be prevented by: (a) withholding of nuclear weapons from countries not now possessing them; (b) transfer of nuclear materials for peaceful purposes to be achieved under international arrangements; (c) peaceful nuclear activities subject to inspection; (d) the banning of all nuclear weapons tests under effective verification and control.[10]

The United States' approach stresses arms-control measures and leaves

[9] Earl H. Voss, *Nuclear Ambush.* (Chicago: H. Regnery Co.), 1963, p. 535.
[10] See United States Arms Control and Disarmament Agency, Publication 23, pp. 1-3.

general and complete disarmament as an ultimate objective but one that is not likely to be achieved very soon. The United States sees little point in talking about complete disarmament until these preliminary steps can be agreed upon. In contrast, the Soviet Union has always put the main emphasis upon general and complete disarmament, for which it has a three-stage program. At the first stage it is proposed to destroy all the means of delivering nuclear weapons (rockets, bombers, submarines and surface ships carrying nuclear weapons, and atomic artillery), dismantle all foreign bases and withdraw all foreign troops in other countries, reduce the armed forces of states and carry out a number of other disarmament measures. At the second stage, to ban nuclear weapons and destroy all their stockpiles, and also the stockpiles of all other types of mass destruction weapons, and to make a further reduction in the armed forces of states. At the third stage, to complete the disbanding of the armed forces and destruction of armaments, to dissolve all military organizations, and to stop military training and budget appropriations for military purposes.[11] The elimination of delivery vehicles and of foreign bases in the first stage of the program would, of course, effectively paralyze the NATO countries and prevent the United States from fulfilling its commitments to its allies. Assuming that the Soviet position is stated in this manner for propaganda purposes, it is reasonable to suggest that this is the Soviet way of saying that it has no interest whatsoever in general and complete disarmament. That is why it makes good sense for the United States to continue to press for arms control; it is within the realm of political reality.

International Police Force

Arms control and disarmament both are closely related to the creation of an international police force. On this subject there is a tremendous amount of literature, and there has been a good deal of discussion in the organs of the United Nations. We have seen how the Soviet Union closely linked the creation of an international police force to disarmament in its "troika" proposals. To the questions raised by Henry Cabot Lodge at the Fourteenth General Assembly—what type of international police force should be established, what principles of international law should govern its use, and what internal security forces could each nation keep if the world were to disarm—Khrushchev added the most far-reaching question of all, who will control the force? To go back to the Charter, it was assumed in 1945 that although a U.N. police force would never be used against the Big Five, the

---

[11] *International Affairs,* "U.N.: Rostrum, Forum, Arena," No. 12, December 1963 (Moscow), p. 13.

military situation was such that it was theoretically impossible for any one power, even the U.S., to stand up against a combination of all other powers. Today the military situation is different. No combination of powers at present could possibly challenge the nuclear capacity of either one of the superpowers. Under present international circumstances the Soviet Union and the United States are not going to contribute to or participate in an international police force that might be used against themselves.

There are things, however, that could be done in the way of an international peace force short of the cooperation of the two superpowers. It would be quite possible to establish a permanent force instead of using the *ad hoc* arrangements that the Secretary-General has relied upon during the last decade. Those nations which are willing to make a contribution could merely inform the Secretary-General that certain units would always be available whenever needed. This is still short of a truly international force; it is more a combination of international units. It is possible, however, that so long as the two superpowers are unable to use their nuclear forces against each other, this sort of force may be all that is necessary at the present time to prevent the escalation of small wars into big ones—a very important concern of the superpowers. In the meantime, the superpowers will continue, either within the U.N. or without and for their own safety and security, to explore areas of agreement in arms control. The functioning of the small international forces we have just discussed is very closely related to the success of arms-control measures. It is with the problems relating to these two activities that United States policy must be chiefly concerned.

V.

THE SECRETARIAT: ADMINISTRATIVE
OR EXECUTIVE?

The Secretary-General

One of the most dramatic and far-reaching developments in the United Nations has been the evolution of the Secretariat. It has been a stormy growth. All of the Big Five have at one time or another shown irritation with the activities of the Secretary-General. The U.S. was irked with Trygve Lie for his Palestine stand and for his 1950 memorandum on Chinese representation. Britain opposed the Secretary-General's anti-colonial stand. France was highly critical of the Secretary-General and the Organization during its controversy with Algeria. The Government of the Republic of China has always opposed any Secretariat move to replace its representative with one from Peiping. The most bitter and continuing attack yet made against the Secretary-General has come from the Soviet Union. This dispute deserves close attention because it is indicative of the general attitude of the Soviet Union toward the U.N. Organization. The Soviet Union has varied from full support to outright condemnation of the Secretary-General; this policy has varied in direct proportion to what the Soviet Government has considered to be an anti-Soviet and pro-Western orientation of the Secretary-General.

The records of the Dumbarton Oaks and San Francisco conferences on the organization of the United Nations do not reveal any basic differences

55

56

among the major powers on the role of the Secretary-General or the Secretariat. In fact the four participating governments at Dumbarton Oaks readily reached agreement on provisions regarding the functions, powers, and method of selection of the Secretary-General.[1] The Secretariat was to be one of the six principal organs of the United Nations, and the tone of Chapter IV of the Charter clearly stresses the international character of the Secretariat. The Secretary-General was to be selected by the Security Council although the actual appointment comes from the General Assembly. All of the major powers favored this method because it gave each a veto over the selection of the person to serve in this highly important post. Only one part of Chapter IV was the subject of dispute. The Soviet and Ukrainian delegations at San Francisco opposed Article 101 (3), which reads: "The paramount consideration in the employment of the staff and in the determination of the conditions of service shall be the necessity of securing the highest standards of efficiency, competence, and integrity. Due regard shall be paid to the importance of recruiting the staff on as wide a geographical basis as possible." The Communists had wanted proportional representation.

The major powers originally sponsored a proposal that four deputies to the Secretary-General should also be elected by the General Assembly on the recommendation of the Security Council. This reflected efforts to strengthen the office of the Secretary-General and the desire of the major powers, in varying degrees, to safeguard their influence in the new organization by having a veto over these deputies. This proposal was defeated because most countries at the conference thought it more important to safeguard the authority and responsibility of the Secretary-General in his choice of subordinates.[2]

Of all the principal organs of the United Nations, the Secretariat was to have the most pronounced international character, with the exception of the International Court of Justice. There was considerable evidence at San Francisco that the participating governments were aware of the political importance of the Secretariat and of the influence it might have in determining the future work of the Organization. Chapter IV clearly gives the Secretary-General a larger political role than his League counterpart.[3] This had been made abundantly clear under the old League of Nations. Sir Eric Drummond made his role much bigger than the Covenant intended it to be. This is, of course, the primary reason for the major powers' insistence on the right of veto in the selection of the Secretary-General. The political role of the Sec-

---

[1] Leland M. Goodrich, *The United Nations* (New York: Crowell, 1959) pp. 132-33.
[2] *Ibid.*, p. 136.
[3] *Ibid.*, p. 113.

retary-General as it has evolved was the focal point of the Soviet opposition to Mr. Trygve Lie and Mr. Dag Hammarskjold.

Trygve Lie

The Soviet Union strongly supported Trygve Lie as the first Secretary-General of the United Nations. Andrei Gromyko nominated Lie for the position, thus creating a false impression, particularly in the United States, that he was the "candidate" of the Soviet Union.[4] He clearly was a compromise candidate who "had no calculated plan for developing the political powers of the office of Secretary-General but . . . was determined that the Secretary-General should be a force for peace."[5] Mr. Lie was more than just an administrator. He did in fact concern himself with political questions and took a definite position when he thought the principles of the Charter were at stake.[6] He did this with full knowledge that his actions would bring him into disfavor with one or more of the great powers.

Until 1950 Mr. Lie received substantial support from the Soviet Union. The Soviet delegate wrote the text of a Security Council resolution which empowered the Secretary-General to intervene in Security Council proceedings at his own discretion and without having to wait to be invited to do so. This was an important addition to the political power of the Secretary-General. The Soviets supported Mr. Lie on the Palestine partition problem when he threatened to resign because of the positions taken by the United States and Great Britain. Gromyko urged him to remain until he could consult with his government, for the Soviet Union felt that Lie was the only man Moscow would support for this position.[7] In 1950, when Lie presented his Twenty Year Program for Achieving Peace through the United Nations, the Soviet Union did not publicly indicate its displeasure even though Lie was told by Molotov in May 1950 that his ideas were quite one-sided. "It contained the Anglo-American point of view and omitted proposals and opinions put forward by the USSR."[8]

The Secretary-General serves for a five-year term, and Mr. Lie's first term was due to expire in February 1951. As early as October 1, 1949, Vyshinsky told Lie at a dinner party in New York that he was the only man the Soviet Union would support. In January 1950 the Soviet Government informed the Norwegian Government of its intention to support Mr. Lie for another term,

---

[4] Trygve Lie, *In the Cause of Peace* (New York: Macmillan, 1954), p. 10.
[5] *Ibid.*, p. 42.
[6] Sydney D. Bailey, "The Troika and the Future of the U.N.," *International Conciliation,* May 1962, pp. 37-38.
[7] Lie, *op. cit.*, p. 171.
[8] *Ibid.*, p. 297.

and this was announced in Moscow on May 15, 1950.[9] The North Korean attack and subsequent United Nations actions to put down this aggression ended Soviet support of Trygve Lie. On July 8, 1950, a Soviet magazine published a scathing article under the title "The Greatness and Decline of Trygve Lie." The Soviet position was that "when he supported the illegal resolution of the United Nations Security Council on the Korean question, Trygve Lie, whose mission it is to protect the peace, took on the role of an accessory to the American aggressors."[10] A *Pravda* article of July 13, 1950, indicated that in "dropping his mask, Mr. Trygve Lie . . . became one of the direct active accomplices of United States armed intervention in Korea."

The changed attitude on Trygve Lie after the outbreak of the Korean War is summarized best in a letter from Andrei Gromyko to the United Nations on July 13, 1950:

> It is impossible not to note the unseemly role played in that whole affair [passage of Korean resolution by the Security Council] by the United Nations Secretary-General, Mr. Trygve Lie. Being under the obligation, by virtue of his position, to observe the exact fulfillment of the United Nations Charter, the Secretary General, during discussion of the Korean question in the Security Council, far from fulfilling his direct duties, on the contrary obsequiously helped a gross violation of the Charter on the part of the United States Government and other members of the Security Council. Thereby the Secretary-General showed that he is concerned not so much with strengthening the United Nations and with promoting peace as with how to help the United States ruling circles to carry out their aggressive plans with regard to Korea.[11]

In the fall of 1950 the Soviet attack on Mr. Lie intensified. The Security Council in October considered his reappointment as Secretary-General for another five-year term, but the Soviet Government vetoed this action. The united stand of the non-Communist members in support of Trygve Lie culminated in the adoption by the General Assembly of a resolution extending his term of office for three years. The Soviet representative on the Security Council, Mr. Malik, concluded his arguments against the appointment by stating that "if the appointment of Mr. Lie is imposed, the USSR will not take Mr. Lie into account and will not consider him as Secretary-General of the United Nations."[12]

---

[9] *Ibid.*, pp. 367-69.

[10] *Ibid.*

[11] United Nations Security Council Document S/1603, July 14, 1950, Supplement for June-July-August 1950, p. 86.

[12] Quoted in Lie, *op. cit.*, p. 382.

The Soviet attitude towards Mr. Lie became more embittered when the Uniting for Peace Resolution was adopted. Mr. Vyshinsky presented the view of the Soviet Union:

> This provision [U.N. armed forces] is basically and fundamentally incompatible with the Charter. It short-circuits the Military Staff Committee and the Security Council. . . . It is even more bizarre than that; it speaks of military experts and advisers who it suggests . . . will be under the orders of the Secretary-General.
>
> Apparently, the military experts will be at the beck and call of the Secretary-General. He is to be commander-in-chief of the armed forces of the General Assembly . . . riding on a white horse. . . .
>
> However, under the Charter, the Secretary-General can only command his workers in the Secretariat. . . . He does not have military experts with or without special panels. He has mimeograph machines. . . . One does not need military experts to run mimeograph machines. . . .[13]

As will be shown later, the Soviet Union objected to the Secretary-General having any authority over actual or potential United Nations military forces on the grounds that the Secretariat was necessarily partial. The Soviet view has not yet been modified on this point.

The Soviet Government kept its promise to ignore the Secretary-General. From February 5, 1951, until Mr. Lie gave up his office on April 10, 1953, the Soviet Union boycotted the man and the office. All correspondence from the Soviet Union was addressed to the Secretariat, not to Mr. Lie or to the Secretary-General.[14] In the Soviet view the job and the man did not exist so long as Mr. Lie was involved. Mr. Lie frankly admits in his memoirs that this disharmony was too great a risk for the future of the Organization, and on November 10, 1952, he announced his resignation. He stated he was leaving the position because he felt it essential that his post be filled by a person in whom all of the major powers had confidence.[15]

Lie's resignation was supposedly effective at once. The assumption was that a successor could be quickly chosen, since the Soviet Union was anxious to rid the Organization of Mr. Lie. The search for a successor was not easy owing to the deep split between the Communist and the Western world. The latter supported Lester Pearson of Canada, who was vetoed by the Soviet Union on March 13, 1953. The Soviet candidate, the Polish foreign minister, was unacceptable to the West. A compromise Secretary-General was

---

[13] *Ibid.,* pp. 346-47.
[14] *Ibid.,* pp. 407-08.
[15] *Ibid.,* p. 407.

finally selected in the person of Dag Hammarskjold of Sweden, who assumed the office on April 10, 1953.

Dag Hammarskjold

Dag Hammarskjold had a dynamic concept of the role of the United Nations and the Secretary-Generalship, which he expressed in action. In time he came into direct conflict with the Soviet Union, and the attack on him was even more bitter and more radical than the earlier attack on Trygve Lie. This intensified attack undoubtedly reflected the increase in responsibilities of the Secretary-General in the political, economic, and social fields.[16]

Like Mr. Lie, Hammarskjold initially had no trouble with the Soviet Union. During the Suez crisis of 1956, the Soviet Union indicated its approval of the actions of the Secretary-General. On October 13, 1956, the Soviet representative on the Security Council stated:

> We are gratified to find that, as a result of the exchange of views between the Ministers of Foreign Affairs of the United Kingdom, France, and Egypt, and with the active and fruitful participation of the Secretary-General of the United Nations, Mr. Hammarskjold, it has become possible to agree on a number of general principles to serve as the basis for working out specific methods and devising appropriate machinery for the peaceful settlement of the Suez question.[17]

Again on October 31, 1956, the Soviet representative made an even stronger statement in support of Hammarskjold when he said: "May I begin by saying that the Soviet delegation has confidence in the Secretary-General of the United Nations and lends him its support."[18] This attitude prevailed when Mr. Hammarskjold was re-elected Secretary-General on September 26, 1957.

The first Soviet objections to Hammarskjold as Secretary-General occurred in 1959, when the United Nations established, over Soviet objections, a fact-finding subcommittee on Laos. The Secretary-General personally went to Laos to help establish "a United Nations presence." The Soviet delegate, Arkadi Sobolev, wrote to Hammarskjold that he should not go there and had no authority to station a representative there. "All such steps cannot be considered otherwise than attempts to use the United Nations for covering the actions of certain powers."[19] This allegation became the central

---

[16] Bailey, *op. cit.*, p. 4.

[17] United Nations Security Council Official Records, 11th Year, 742d meeting, October 13, 1956, p. 12.

[18] United Nations Security Council Official Records, 11th Year, 751st meeting, October 31, 1956, p. 2.

[19] Quoted in Dallin, *op. cit.*, p. 129.

argument of the Soviet Union against the Secretary-General during the Congo crisis of 1960-61.

It is doubtful whether the decision of the Soviet Government to attack Hammarskjold and to propose drastic reforms in the structure of the United Nations was based primarily on one or two incidents in the Congo situation. The Soviet Union supported the first three resolutions asking the Secretary-General to implement the Security Council decisions.[20] These resolutions, however, dealt with the prevention of a Belgian take-over. The withdrawal of Belgian troops became the first objective of the United Nations. The goal of eliminating foreign interference was set in the second resolution.

> As for the nature of the U.N. task . . . the U.N. action would not be an enforcement action under Articles 41 and 42, against an aggressor. It was not the Korean precedent that was being followed, but the precedents of all the other operations in which the U.N. had acted not as a soldier but as a fireman. The precise legal basis of the United Nations intervention was not made clear (and remains in doubt) but the political nature was unmistakable.[21]

It appears more likely that what really disturbed the Soviet Government was the general trend that the United Nations was taking.

As suggested earlier, there had been an increase in the responsibilities of the Secretary-General, and two of these trends are of special interest. First, the policymaking organs of the United Nations had increasingly entrusted the Secretary-General with broad diplomatic and operational functions. Second, the Secretary-General was using all the resources of his office in the exercise of independent initiative designed to further the purposes and principles of the Charter.[22] These two trends became more objectionable to the Soviet Union as the responsibility and influence of the Security Council for maintenance of peace and security declined.

Hammarskjold took the view that the recommendations of the General Assembly tended more and more to be recognized as decisions having weight and binding effect, particularly when they involved the application of the principles of the Charter and of international law.[23] The application of these principles on an impartial basis would thwart Soviet foreign policy objectives particularly as pursued within the United Nations. Thus the Soviet attack on Hammarskjold was not primarily directed at any specific and consistent

---

[20] Bailey, *op. cit.*, pp. 47-48.
[21] Stanley Hoffman, "The U.N. in the Congo Labyrinth," *International Organization,* Spring 1962, p. 333.
[22] Bailey, *op. cit.*, p. 44.
[23] *Ibid.*, p. 11.

doctrine that he was expressing but rather at the implications of his actions for the future development of the United Nations. If Hammarskjold were not checked, perhaps the Organization might become too effective. The total development of the Secretary-Generalship had clearly given it a character not foreseen by the founders of the United Nations. The Soviet Union concluded it must take drastic action to halt the general trend of developments in the Organization.

Khrushchev himself carried the main attack against the Secretary-General when he appeared at the Fifteenth Session of the General Assembly from September 19 to October 13, 1960. The theme was repeated many times, and the bitterness of the attack remained constant. Khrushchev's main arguments were that the United Nations forces in the Congo—though sent legally —had exceeded their powers by interfering in Congolese domestic affairs, that Dag Hammarskjold was the willing assistant of the colonialists, that the executive machinery of the United Nations should be replaced by a three-man secretariat (the "troika"), and that an agreement on disarmament and a permanent United Nations military force was impossible until Soviet demands were met.[24]

The Soviet Premier claimed his objections to Hammarskjold were not personal but were made to "call Mr. Hammarskjold to order so that he should not abuse his position as Secretary-General and should discharge his duties in strict conformity with the provisions of the United Nations Charter and decisions of the Security Council."[25] The Soviet leader objected to Hammarskjold's "pursuing the line of the colonialists" and in "opposing the legitimate Government of the Congo and the Congolese people" and in "supporting the renegades who under the guise of fighting for the independence of the Republic of the Congo are in fact continuing the policy of the colonialists and are apparently getting remuneration from them for their treachery."[26]

Specifically, the development which disturbed the Soviet Union most was Dag Hammarskjold's implementation of the broad objectives handed him by the Security Council or the General Assembly. The practice had developed in the Organization that when it was not possible to muster sufficient votes either in the Security Council or the General Assembly for any proposal of substance, members usually were content to transfer the responsibility for action to the Secretary-General by declaring in broad terms the objectives to be achieved and leaving the details to the Secretary-General.[27] Hammar-

[24] *Khrushchev in New York* (New York: Crosscurrents Press, 1960), pp. 22-59.
[25] *Ibid.*, p. 22.
[26] *Ibid.*, p. 52.
[27] Bailey, *op. cit.*, p. 44.

skjold did not hesitate to use his powers and to make the decisions he felt necessary for the preservation of peace. Most members of the Organization were glad to have a man of his skill and stature; that is why they turned to him when other methods failed. In fulfilling the tasks entrusted to him, Hammarskjold had significant advantages: the high prestige attached to his office, his own personal integrity, courage, tact and skill, and the respect with which he was held by most delegations.[28] He had acted decisively in the Congo when he ordered United Nations forces to prevent hostilities between the competing Congolese factions. He believed the risks of big-power intervention were a greater threat to the peace than any action he might take to restore law and order to the Congo.

The Soviet Challenge

Khrushchev made his famous "troika" proposal to prevent international action which might be detrimental to Soviet interests.

We consider it expedient to set up instead of a Secretary-General who is presently the interpreter and executor of the Assembly and Security Council decisions, a collective executive body of the United Nations comprising three persons each of whom would represent a certain group of states. A definite guarantee would thereby be created that the work of the United Nations executive would not be conducted to the detriment of any of these groups of states. Then the United Nations executive will really be a democratic body, it will really safeguard the interests of all United Nations member states irrespective of the social and political systems of the various states making up the United Nations. This is particularly necessary at the present time, and will be the more so in the future.[29]

The three groups of states mentioned by Khrushchev are the "military" blocs of the Western powers, the socialist states, and neutral countries. Although it was never clearly stated in the Soviet proposal, presumably each of these bloc representatives would have a veto power over Secretariat action. If adopted, the "troika" would prevent future United Nations actions which were opposed by the Soviet Union or the United States. It would deprive the United Nations of an executive agent to carry out the resolutions of the Security Council and the General Assembly. It would emasculate the Organization and defeat with finality the stated purposes of the Charter.

Mr. Khrushchev reiterated that he was not opposed to Hammarskjold per-

[28] *Ibid.*
[29] *Khrushchev in New York, op. cit.*, p. 53.

sonally but was "looking for a more perfect form of organization that would guarantee peaceful coexistence of all states."[30] In fact, Khrushchev volunteered that the Soviet Union would cooperate with Mr. Hammarskjold as the representative of the Western bloc provided the other two blocs had a representative.

> We are not in favor of substituting our own candidate for Hammarskjold. You cannot find a man for this post who would be three groups of states at once. That just cannot be done. True, they say that God was three in one. But nobody has ever seen Him. So let Him remain in the imaginations of believers. What we want to have is a three-man U.N. Secretariat.[31]

The "troika" proposal was closely linked with the structure of the Secretariat, with disarmament, and with the establishment of international armed forces which would be employed under United Nations orders. As part of his argument for revision of the Secretariat, Khrushchev indicated that the Soviet Union would not agree to the creation of international armed forces if such forces were to be under the "sole command" of the United Nations Secretary-General. Khrushchev bluntly stated that without the three-man Secretariat it would not be possible for the major powers to agree on a commander of any international military forces under the present one-man Secretary-General. In September 1961 Mr. Khrushchev made a distinction between disarmament and an international military force.

> Khrushchev told C. I. Sulzberger that "in setting up disarmament controls there should be no veto and no troika. . . ." The trioka principle will be necessary only in the event that international forces are set up. The command of these forces should be based on that principle. This would be necessary to guarantee that no state or group of states could use international United Nations forces to the detriment of any other state or group of states.[32]

Sydney D. Bailey, former Director of the Quaker United Nations Program, believes it significant that the "troika system was linked closely to possible future developments in relation to disarmament and the peace-keeping functions of the United Nations."[33] The Soviet Union has indicated quite clearly that there will be no international military forces unless such forces can be controlled by the Soviets through a three-man Secretariat.

---

[30] *Ibid.,* p. 103.
[31] *Ibid.*
[32] Quoted in Bailey, *op. cit.,* p. 53
[33] *Ibid.,* p. 49.

Soviet demands varied all the way from the "troika" proposal to suggestions that Hammarskjold resign or be dismissed from his post. The Soviets used the death of Patrice Lumumba on February 12, 1961 as a pretext for stiffening their attitude.

> The murder of Patrice Lumumba and his comrade-in-arms . . . is the culmination of Hammarskjold's criminal activities. Dag Hammarskjold must be dismissed from the post of Secretary-General as a participant in and organizer of the violence committed against the leading statesmen of the Republic of the Congo which has sullied the name of the United Nations.[34]

The United Nations thus returned to 1950; insofar as the Soviet Government was concerned, the Secretary-General did not exist.

This Soviet statement meant that the Soviet Union would pursue its now established policy of ignoring the Secretary-General. The issue never came to a climax, however, because Dag Hammarskjold was killed in Africa in September 1961 while trying to reconcile conflicting groups in the Congo. His death raised the possibility that the Soviets would now insist upon the "troika" arrangement for the Secretary-General. It was obvious that the Soviet viewpoint would not be accepted by the vast majority of the United Nations, and agreement was reached on a temporary Secretary-General in the person of U Thant of Burma. U Thant was appointed Acting Secretary-General on November 3, 1961, and was to serve until April 10, 1963. This appointment ended the major Soviet effort to establish the "troika." It may be important to note that Soviet protests about important decisions between the death of Hammarskjold and the appointment of U Thant were relatively perfunctory. It is not possible at this juncture to state with finality that the Soviet Union has abandoned its efforts to establish a "troika"-type Secretariat. It seems certain that the proposal has been shelved for the moment and can be resurrected at any time it suits the convenience of the Soviet Union.

The Soviet attack on the Secretary-General went far beyond a mere personal attack on Trygve Lie or Dag Hammarskjold. The essential points in the Soviet position appear to be: (1) the United Nations has developed into a more effective body than the Soviet Union anticipated or desires; (2) the Soviet Government cannot tolerate any U.N. organ, especially the Secretariat, which may take action in opposition to Soviet foreign policy; (3) the Soviet Union feels that its overall strength requires even representation with the Western nations in all components of the United Nations; and (4) the notion

---

[34] United Nations Security Council Official Records, 16th Year, Supplement for January-February-March 1961. U.N. Document S/4704, p. 115.

66

of an international civil service is a myth and a hoax behind which the Western "imperialistic" powers manipulate the United Nations to promote their own policies.[35]

The Soviet Union is also concerned with the increasing effectiveness of the United Nations and its specialized agencies in the economic and social fields; the success of such work could be a serious challenge to long-range Soviet objectives. It is important to remember that the Secretary-General plays a key role in this area because he is the key permanent official of the United Nations in all of its major organs.

U Thant

The Soviet Union failed in its efforts to discredit the Secretary-General and to secure fundamental changes in the organization of the Secretariat. The Soviet Government apparently accepts defeat for the moment since it did approve U Thant's appointment as the regular Secretary-General. *The Economist* summed it up as follows:

> The day before Mr. Thant's re-election, the Soviet bloc suffered a resounding defeat in the U.N. Assembly's administrative committee, which voted by 84 to 10 in support of his [U Thant's] proposals for future staff recruitments, sweeping aside Russia's renewed demands for the reshaping of the whole Secretariat on a three-bloc basis. As to the Secretary-General himself, the Russians have had to abandon all hope of tying strings onto his freedom of decision.[36]

U Thant of Burma, like his predecessors, comes from a neutral country. His election as Secretary-General (November 30, 1962), which came mainly as a consequence of the deadlock between Washington and Moscow, was also due to the rising political import of the Afro-Asian states, a probable source for future Secretary-Generals. Like his predecessors, U Thant has looked on his role as an active and positive one. In the Congo crisis he urged members of the U.N. to use economic pressure to persuade Katanga to give up its claims to independence and opposed any solution short of the reunification of the Congo. He went far beyond the August 1960 resolution of the Security Council that the U.N. could not be a party to an internal political problem. U.N. forces withdrew in June 1964, but the validity of the role played by the Secretary-General and the U.N. is still open to question.

U Thant did not hesitate to state his views on the Cuba missile crisis of

[35] Bailey, *op. cit.,* p. 49.
[36] "Better Mouse-Trap," *The Economist,* December 8, 1962.

October 1962. He went to Cuba and talked with Castro but was unable to convince him to allow U.N. inspectors to witness the removal of the missiles. That the issue remained outside U.N. jurisdiction was not due to any reluctance on the part of the Secretary-General. Although the treaty was negotiated outside the U.N., U Thant was present in Moscow at the signing of the partial Nuclear Test Ban Treaty in 1963. The Secretary-General was also active in the negotiations during the Nineteenth Session of the General Assembly concerning the question of U.N. financing. He was particularly anxious to avoid a direct U.S.-U.S.S.R. confrontation over the application of Article 19.

Thus far the third Secretary-General has not been attacked by the Soviet Union, and there is every reason to believe that he will be re-elected to this post, probably in the fall of 1965. The Soviet Union would find it difficult, of course, to accuse the present Secretary-General of a pro-Western stand without the risk of offending simultaneously other representatives of the Afro-Asian nations.

Much of the future discussion of the U.N. Organization will revolve around the role of the Secretary-General for the very good reason that this office has come to symbolize the U.N. as an active and sometimes effective agent for keeping the peace as well as the driving force behind the work of the U.N. in those social and economic fields which are so important to the new nations.

Dag Hammarskjold was the first Secretary-General to understand the psychological and political influence of a U.N. "presence." This "presence" might be a personal representative of the Secretary-General, as in Jordan and Laos; a mixed armistice commission to prevent armed clashes, as in the Gaza strip between the Israelis and the Arabs; or a U.N. emergency force of considerable size, as in Egypt (1956), the Congo (1960-64), or Cyprus (1964). Hammarskjold was strongly in favor of permanent regional and local offices for U.N. representatives all over the world in order to persuade the peoples of the world that the U.N. was interested in their problems— that it was, in other words, a going concern. U Thant has carried on this Hammarskjold tradition. The growth of the initiative of the Secretary-General has been due to the failure of the Security Council and the General Assembly to make decisions when faced with serious questions. He has filled a vacuum. In all likelihood this situation may continue, but it is possible that the office of Secretary-General may again become a political issue. It is not so much, perhaps, the office of the Secretary-General that is at issue—even the big powers see the value of the office in preventing the escalation of small wars—as the role. Is the office to be controlled by the Security Council or the General Assembly? By the big powers or the small ones? Or is there a compromise slightly more favorable to the small powers than the one they had to accept at San Francisco?

The International Civil Service

The Secretary-General cannot do the massive United Nations administrative job alone. He depends upon a corps of multi-national civil servants who are expected to serve the United Nations in an impartial and constructive manner. These international employees, unlike members of national delegations, are supposedly influenced by international considerations rather than by the emotions and prejudices of national policies. This is not to say that they must sever all ties of loyalty to their own nations; rather it means that they will examine the questions before them on an institutional basis and not be unduly influenced by the aspirations of their own country. International civil servants do not act in a vacuum. The Charter in Article 100 established the framework for the United Nations staff:

1. In the performance of their duties the Secretary-General and the staff shall not seek or receive instructions from any government or from any other authority external to the Organization. They shall refrain from any action which might reflect on their position as international officials responsible only to the Organization.

2. Each member of the United Nations undertakes to respect the exclusively international character of the responsibilities of the Secretary-General and the staff and not to seek to influence them in the discharge of their responsibilities.

How has this concept worked in action? As with all other U.N. activities, the Secretariat has become embroiled in the cold war. The Soviet Union openly challenges the basic tenet of Article 100 by denying even the possibility of an impartial civil service. The late Dag Hammarskjold summarized the Soviet position in the following terms:

In a recent article Mr. Walter Lippmann tells about an interview in Moscow with Mr. Khrushchev. According to the article, Chairman Khrushchev stated that "while there are neutral countries, there are no neutral men," and the author draws the conclusion that it is now the view of the Soviet government "that there can be no such thing as an impartial civil servant in this deeply divided world, and that the kind of political celibacy which the British theory of the civil servant calls for is, in international affairs, a fiction." [37]

In practice, Soviet nationals who serve in the Secretariat represent the Soviet Government and make no serious effort to adopt an impartial attitude. When the Secretariat is called upon to make key political decisions in crises such as the Congo, the Soviet member must be by-passed, for he will place many obstacles in the way if the decision being contemplated does not coincide with official Soviet policy.

The United States record has not been one of consistent support for the concept of an impartial international civil service as understood by the U.N. Secretariat. The U.S. took a strong stand during the early 1950's against the U.N. employing, or continuing to employ, U.S. nationals who had allegedly engaged in subversive activities. This U.S. stand has been described, somewhat melodramatically, as the "most overt threat to the principles of Articles 100 and 101." [38] The Secretary-General finally accepted the U.S. view that no one should be employed by the organization if "there was substantial evidence indicating subversive activities directed against his own or any other State." [39] What really disturbed the Secretariat, however, was the possibility that a member could prevent the employment of any person merely because he had questioned or disapproved of the policy of his government. The Secretary-General claimed that national investigations of international officials would dilute Article 101 and subsequent General Assembly resolutions which placed full authority in his hands for appointment of staff members. Measures taken by the U.S. included the investigation of non-American international officials, the questioning and fingerprinting of U.S. nationals in the headquarters building itself, and the refusal to issue passports to some U.S. citizens in U.N. employment. [40] Partly because of the "resolute and courageous attitude of certain national governments and certain heads of international secretariats," [41] partly because of growing confidence in the Secretariat, the U.S. was able to work out arrangements more or less acceptable to both sides and the crisis came to an end.

Premier Khrushchev raised a question concerning the composition of the

[37] Dag Hammarskjold, *The International Civil Service in Law and in Fact* (Oxford: Clarendon Press, 1961), p. 3.
[38] Sydney D. Bailey, *The Secretariat of the United Nations* (New York: Carnegie Endowment for International Peace, 1962), p. 26.
[39] *Ibid.*
[40] Georges Langrod, *The International Civil Service* (Leiden: A. W. Sythoff, 1963), pp. 225-26.
[41] *Ibid.*, p. 229.

Secretariat in his tirade against the Secretary-General during his appearance before the General Assembly in 1960. Krushchev asserted that:

> . . . the executive machinery of the Organization is . . . constituted partially. It often approaches the solution of questions from the standpoint of a certain group of countries. This is particularly true of the activities of the United Nations Secretary-General. As a rule the Western countries that make up the military blocs of the Western powers exploit this post in their interests by nominating for the post of United Nations Secretary-General a candidate that is acceptable to themselves. The result is that in many cases the practical routine work of the United Nations and of its Secretariat is in effect carried out one-sidedly. The personnel of the Organization is picked one-sidedly as well.[42]

It is true that the staff of the United Nations Secretariat as of April 1, 1961, consisted of 44 Soviet citizens including one Under Secretary-General, 131 British subjects including one Under Secretary-General, and 355 Americans including three Under Secretaries-General.[43] But this disparity reflects the essential fact that the two Western nations concerned have many more *qualified* persons to fill the vacancies in the United Nations Secretariat. The Soviet Government has admitted perhaps disingenuously that it does not have enough qualified persons to fill a large number of positions in international organizations.[44]

The United Nations established a Committee of Experts on the Activities and Organization of the Secretariat. The Committee recommended a gradual increase in the number of non-Western nationals in the international civil service. Not only would the Soviet Union be expected to provide additional trained personnel, but the newly-emerged and underdeveloped countries would be expected to provide personnel for international organs as they were trained and became available. If these recommendations are implemented, and if the Soviet Union provides more personnel, much of the Soviet argument concerning the unrepresentative character of the Secretariat could be eliminated. It is not likely to be eliminated because the Soviet Union is not willing to invest qualified men in the U.N. and if it did they would serve solely the interests of the Soviet Union. The Soviet Union does not believe that an impartial international civil service is either possible or desirable.

---

[42] See *Khrushchev in New York, op. cit.*, pp. 50-51.
[43] Report of the Committee of Experts on the Activities and Organization of the Secretariat, U.N. Document A/4776.
[44] Dallin, *op. cit.*, chapter 8.

The late Dag Hammarskjold had strong views on the problem and of the consequences if it is not solved. Speaking at Oxford he said:

Recently it has been said, this time in Western circles, that as the International Secretariat goes forward on the road of international thought and action, while Member States depart from it, a gap develops between them and they grow into mutually hostile elements; and this is said to increase the tension in the world which it was the purpose of the United Nations to diminish. From this view the conclusion has been drawn that we may have to switch from an international Secretariat, ruled by the principles described in this lecture, to an intergovernmental Secretariat, the members of which obviously would not be supposed to work in the direction of an internationalism considered unpalatable to their governments. Such a passive acceptance of a nationalism rendering it necessary to abandon present efforts in the direction of internationalism symbolized by the international civil service—somewhat surprisingly regarded as a cause of tension—might, if accepted by the Member Nations, well prove to be the Munich of international cooperation as conceived after the First World War and further developed under the impression of the tragedy of the Second World War. To abandon or to compromise with principles on which such cooperation is built may be no less dangerous than to compromise with principles regarding the rights of a nation. In both cases the price to be paid may be peace.[45]

The core of an international civil service based on merit is already in being, as Hammarskjold pointed out. It is made up of those who come from nations which share, to a significant extent, the same values and purposes. It owes much to the tradition of the League of Nations, especially its technical services. The example that it sets has a moral and political influence that should not be underestimated; it gains by comparison with the behavior of those U.N. officials who first and foremost serve their own countries. From the point of view of developing the U.N. as well as of discrediting Communist motives there is every reason for the U.S. to support the Secretary-General in building up a competent and impartial civil service.

[45] Hammarskjold, *op. cit.*, pp. 27-28.

VI.

ECONOMIC, SOCIAL, CULTURAL, AND HUMANITARIAN FUNCTION

Economic and Social Functions

Aims and Organization

The second major function of the United Nations is to "achieve international cooperation in solving problems of an economic, social, cultural, or humanitarian character," and to promote and encourage respect for "human rights and for fundamental freedoms for all" (Article 1 and Chapter X of the Charter). The emphasis in the Charter on the importance of international, economic, and social cooperation, though unprecedented in its scope, has its origins in earlier cooperative efforts to solve multi-national problems, such as the International Telegraphic Union, the Universal Postal Union, and other undertakings in the fields of labor, agriculture, health, and transportation. The League of Nations accomplished in its lifetime far more in these fields than was anticipated in the Covenant. As Professor Leland M. Goodrich of Columbia suggests, the effective work of the League in furthering economic and social welfare had proved so valuable that an attempt was made—although too late—"to reorganize the League as an organization for the promotion of economic and social cooperation. It was thought that it might continue to do its useful work in this field even though

73

74

for all practical purposes the League had ceased to function as an organization to keep the peace.[1]

The writing of the Charter provisions on economic and social cooperation proved as difficult as those pertaining to the preservation of peace and security and to the special veto privilege granted to the military giants. The United States committed itself early in the preliminary discussions with Britain and the Soviet Union to the concept of postwar cooperation to deal with common economic and social problems. The interrelationship of domestic economies was clearly recognized. The United States was probably more optimistic than the other Western nations about what could be achieved in this area.

The Soviet Union did not want the postwar Organization to have any social or economic functions. Soviet representatives stressed that the United Nations should not endanger its main task of peace-keeping by multiplying its tasks. Moscow finally yielded to Western pressures to include these functions within the United Nations framework, but this did not mean she would take part in any or all of them. For the first ten years she was not interested in the many social, economic, and cultural activities of the United Nations.[2] Other writers have put it even more strongly:

> Communists have generally refused to join the efforts of other groups or nations for social improvement and the alleviation of misery. They have exploited human suffering for purposes of political power, even to the point of aggravating or engendering suffering for the end of their political advancements.[3]

Soviet agreement to the inclusion of economic and social functions indicated the Soviet expectation that the Organization would not develop into an effective institution. The "limited view of the United Nations functions harmonizes with Moscow's insistence on the broadest interpretation of national sovereignty on the part of member nations and the great powers in particular, and with Moscow's desire to reserve for itself the greatest possible freedom of action."[4] To a great extent, the Charter provisions in the social, economic, cultural, and humanitarian fields reflect the Soviet reservations.

The General Assembly is the organ responsible for initiating studies, making recommendations, setting up programs, and urging members to

---

[1] Goodrich, *op. cit.,* p. 263.
[2] Dallin, *op. cit.,* p. 22.
[3] Niemeyer and Reshetar, *op. cit.,* pp. 65-66.
[4] Dallin, *op. cit.,* p. 22

cooperate. Whatever decisions are made or whatever the type and scope of resolution adopted by this Assembly, *they are recommendations only— not legislation—and cannot be enforced within the territory of any state.* Nothing can be accomplished in these fields unless funds are available, and neither the General Assembly nor any other United Nations organ has the power to tax. Critics of the United Nations often ignore this essential fact or give the General Assembly a power it clearly does not have. The Charter (Article 55) provides that the United Nations shall promote higher standards of living, full employment, economic and social progress and development, solutions of international economic, social, and health problems, and universal respect for and observance of human rights. Like the peace-keeping provision, these are pledges of intention only and can be accepted or rejected by each member at will. A certain amount of activity has been undertaken in these vast areas.

What has been accomplished has resulted from the work of the Economic and Social Council and the various specialized agencies. It was obvious to the writers of the Charter that the General Assembly did not have the time or talent to solve these basic problems. Thus a third major organ of the United Nations was established: an Economic and Social Council, which has broad responsibilities to initiate projects in economic, social, cultural, educational, and health matters, but may only recommend that the General Assembly adopt its product. On this council there are 18 representatives who serve for three-year terms. There was no provision made for any permanent members, but in practice the Big Five until recently have always been elected and re-elected to this organ, the exception being the representative of China, who has not been re-elected to the Economic and Social Council since 1963. In contrast with the Security Council, there is no veto. There is little doubt that the Economic and Social Council was intended to develop into a major international force, but its efforts were limited because its membership has generally overrepresented the more industrially developed nations. The work of the Economic and Social Council can be expected to increase as more underdeveloped nations assume their place in the United Nations.

What are some of the achievements and failures? A partial listing of the commissions and boards created by this council indicates the breadth of its activities: The Transport and Communications Commission, the Statistical Commission, the Social Commission, the Commission on Narcotic Drugs, the Human Rights Commission, the Technical Assistance Committee, and the United Nations Children's Fund. There are also four regional economic commissions (Latin America, Africa, Europe, and Asia and the Far East) which "undertake research and advise the Council on problems of a regional nature and make direct recommendations to member governments, governments admitted in an advisory capacity, and specialized agencies on matters falling within their competence." [5] There is no general agreement that these regional commissions have been successful in performing constructive work in the economic field. Ideally, as Mr. Goodrich suggests, they are closer to the problems of their respective areas, "they have been responsive to them, and have on the whole dealt with them to the satisfaction of both the countries of the region and outside members. Furthermore, they have stimulated a spirit of self-help in meeting regional problems." [6] In practice the record is definitely uneven, and in some countries, especially in Latin America, particularly controversial. Instead of encouraging self-help, many of the activities of the Economic Commission for Latin America, according to competent observers, have achieved the opposite. Greater attention will have to be paid to these regional commissions if they are to play a useful role in the economic development of new members of the United Nations Organization. In this regard, the United States' Point Four Program initiated during President Truman's Administration has served as the basis for the United Nations' Expanded Program for Technical Assistance. But experience has shown that the doctrines on which American foreign aid is based need careful reexamination if the economic and political ends it is supposed to serve are to be achieved.[7]

Much of the work of the United Nations has been done by the specialized agencies, some of which existed before the United Nations itself, or even the League of Nations. They are expected to bring about international cooperation in the economic, social, and humanitarian areas. These specialized agencies have a direct relationship to the United Nations through a special agreement which brings their work under the general supervision of the Economic and Social Council. Today there are 13 specialized agencies: the Universal Postal Union, the International Telecommunications Union, the International Civil Aviation Organization, the World Meteorological Organization, the Food and Agricultural Organization, the International Monetary Fund, the International Bank for Reconstruction and Development, the United Nations Educational, Scientific, and Cultural Organization, the International Labor Organization, the World Health Organization, the International Finance Corporation, the Inter-governmental Maritime Consultative Organization, and the International Development Association. The United

[5] Goodrich, *op. cit.,* p. 272.
[6] *Ibid.*
[7] See Banfield, *op. cit.*

States maintains membership in each of these specialized agencies, and our financial support has been of primary significance in the accomplishment of their missions.

Contributions and Accomplishments

The United States accepts the premise that starvation, disaster, disease, ignorance, and underdevelopment are international problems. Furthermore, the U.S. Government accepts the Food and Agricultural Organization findings that more than half of the world's population suffers from hunger and malnutrition and that this human suffering and human degradation "pose a serious threat to peace and orderly process."[8] The late President Kennedy made the point in his last address before the General Assembly:

The effort to improve the conditions of man, however, is not a task for a few. It is the task of all nations—acting alone, acting in groups, acting in the United Nations—for plague and pestilence, and plunder and pollution, the hazards of nature, and the hunger of children are the foes of every nation. The earth, the sea, and the air are the concern of every nation. And science, technology, and education can be the ally of every nation. Never before has man had such capacity to control his own environment—to end thirst and hunger, to conquer poverty and disease, to banish illiteracy and massive human misery. We have the power to make this the best generation of mankind in the history of the world—or to make it the last.[9]

But even though there is a general American dedication to these propositions, U.S. policymakers are faced with deciding whether the record shows these to be essential functions of the United Nations. In other words, can U.S. assistance to those nations seeking economic viability be channeled best through U.S. channels or should it continue essentially on a bilateral basis? A brief examination of the record may help to clarify the choices.

The central part of the U.N.'s economic program is the Expanded Program of Technical Assistance which was conceived as an international adaptation of President Truman's Point Four Program. President Eisenhower's Administration strongly supported the idea of the U.N. Special Fund which was established in 1957 as a means to provide systematic and sustained financial aid in essential technical, economic, and social fields. President Kennedy suc-

[8] Development Through Food, Freedom From Hunger Campaign, Basic Study No. 2, Food and Agriculture Organization, Rome, 1962.
[9] U.S. Participation in the U.N., Report by the President to the Congress for the Year 1963, Department of State Publication 7675, International Organization and Conference Series 51, August 1964, p. 168.

cessfully urged the U.N. to establish the 1960's as the U.N. Decade of Development, and President Johnson has initiated steps to get the U.N. to merge its technical assistance machinery in order to make the goal of sustained worldwide economic growth a reality. All four Presidents have recognized that the basic principle of technical assistance is that "the less developed countries need not only money and machines, but also skilled manpower. The program is designed to provide skills." [10] Through 1963 the United States has provided nearly $400 million in technical assistance to developing countries through the Expanded Program of Technical Assistance. The United States is the major financial supporter for EPTA, and our 1963 pledge of $21.4 million accounted for 40 percent of the annual total.[11] In 1963, the United States donated $30 million of the total of $75 million budget for the Special Fund. It is important to note that the Expanded Program of Technical Assistance and the Special Fund are financed solely by voluntary contributions of U.N. members.

It would be impossible to list all the activities of the various U.N. economic and technical assistance programs. Even though the list would be impressive, when measured by the great need and the millions of people involved, the results have been modest. Many of the newly independent African countries, such as Morocco, Tunisia, Ghana, and the Congo, have received technical assistance. The World Health Organization, which undertook a worldwide program to eliminate malaria, has been particularly active in India, Pakistan, Afghanistan, Iran, Ceylon, Thailand, and parts of Africa. Tuberculosis teams have operated in many African and Asian countries. There was a campaign against yaws in Nigeria and Liberia. Comprehensive agricultural surveys have been made by the Food and Agricultural Organization experts in Europe, Africa, South America, and Asia. The United Nations Educational, Scientific, and Cultural Organization has launched projects dealing with free primary school education and has initiated a study of semiarid lands from Morocco to India. Money has been loaned to Brazil by the World Bank to construct a vast hydroelectric project, and Thailand has received loans to build a dam near Bangkok.[12]

The United States has supported the cooperative effort under U.N. auspices to develop the irrigation, navigation, and hydroelectric potentialities of the Mekong River in its lower basin, which extends some 1,300 miles and affects Cambodia, Laos, Thailand, and Vietnam. "In addition to the four riparian

---

[10] Stephen S. Fenichell, *The United Nations Design for Peace* (New York: Holt, Rinehart and Winston, 1960), p. 86.

[11] See *U.S. Participation in the U.N., op. cit.,* p. 176.

[12] Fenichell, *op. cit.,* pp. 88-91.

states, sixteen members of the United Nations, including the United States, eleven U.N. agencies, three private foundations, and three private companies are cooperating on the project." [13]   The Economic Commission for Africa was instrumental in the establishment in August 1963 of an African Development Bank to mobilize technical and financial resources.   "Membership, direction, and operation, however, will be exclusively African, and the initial capital will come from the African countries." [14]   The United States continues to be the largest contributor to the United Nations Children's Fund (UNICEF) which, in one view, "has become a symbol of successful U.N. cooperation for the common good." [15]   And yet with all of this activity there is little evidence that the U.N. has moved successfully toward its stated objective of improving the world standard of living.   Improvements in public health and construction of public works and even positive results in improving agricultural and industrial production have not kept up with population growth or lessened the widening gap between the advanced and the backward parts of the world.

One of the most comprehensive economic and technical plans yet approved by the General Assembly (December 1961) is a worldwide food development program known as the Freedom from Hunger Campaign.   Its first task is to distribute food surpluses to food-deficient peoples.   This is not intended to be a gigantic charity program but a very carefully worked out plan to use food as a means to accelerate economic development.[16]   Food received as aid in this program "should be integrated in the over-all development programs of receiving countries and planned in such a way as to maintain adequate balance in the development of their economies"[17] —an over-ambitious assignment in global planning which faces the practical problem of securing the full cooperation and participation of all developed countries.   "Over the period 1957-58 to 1958-59, only one developed country contributed more than 1.4 per cent of its gross national product as public economic aid for bilateral economic assistance to underdeveloped countries (France, 1.4 per cent)." [18]   Aid through multilateral organizations was smaller than that channeled through bilateral arrangements.   This U.N. plan is not intended to prejudice bilateral arrangements; it accepts some measure of international responsibility for solving a worldwide problem.[19] The United

[13] See *U.S. Participation in the U.N.*, *op. cit.*, p. 203.
[14] *Ibid.*, p. 208.
[15] *Ibid.*, p. 230.
[16] F.A.O. Report no. 2, *op. cit.*, p. xi.
[17] *Ibid.*, p. 2.
[18] *Ibid.*, p. 11.
[19] *Ibid.*, p. 121.

States proposes that the United Nations implement the FAO report by the establishment of an initial fund of $100 million, of which this country would contribute $40 million. Whatever may be said about the economic value of the program, participation in it is politically sound.

Foreign Aid Policies

The United Nations has not been heavily involved in U.S. expenditure on foreign aid, which has amounted to over $100 billion since World War II. This aid has taken many forms, including bilateral arrangements between the U.S. and another country (such as the Truman Plan), multilateral arrangements (such as the Marshall Plan), and, more recently, the Alliance for Progress. Foreign aid has been justified as an important arm of U.S. foreign policy having as its general purpose the strengthening of the economies of receiving countries. It is not surprising that there is a considerable amount of disagreement about its efficacy outside Europe, because the problems of Asia, Africa, and Latin America are far more difficult.

What is generally accepted as the official U.S. justification of foreign aid is stated by William Ebenstein in his study *Today's ISMS:*

> The economic aid program is the indirect method of the United States to counteract communism by helping economically retarded nations so that they do not have to look to communist revolution as the way out. Subversion, infiltration, and civil war are the communist methods of preventing underdeveloped societies from evolving peacefully into more advanced social and economic conditions. If India, for example, can show the backward areas throughout the world that it can develop economically while retaining political liberty, it will win the race with China for leadership in Asia. If India stagnates economically, and China progresses, the communists will have convinced Asia that peaceful progress is dubious, and that totalitarian communism is the better road to economic and political-military power.[20]

The assumption is that a blow will have been struck against Communist doctrine if foreign aid succeeds in fostering economic and political conditions in the underdeveloped areas which will allow these nations to survive as independent and free entities.

American critics of the foreign aid program charge that it has been characterized by waste and extravagance and that it has done more harm than good. Some have suggested that foreign aid should go only to U.S. friends.

---

[20] William Ebenstein, *Today's ISMS* (Englewood Cliffs, N.J.: Prentice-Hall, 1964), p. 14.

Others argue that "the American government does not have the right, much less the obligation to try to promote the economic and social welfare of foreign peoples." [21]

George Kennan has questioned the proposition that the developed countries should have "some sort of cosmic guilt or obligation vis-à-vis the under-developed parts of the world." [22] While he does not summarily reject all aid —he supports soundly conceived plans which will yield greater stability and hopefulness for the countries concerned—he believes that foreign aid "cannot be regarded as a very promising device for combating, over the short term, the psychological handicaps under which Western statesmanship now rests in Asia and Africa." [23] This view cannot be lightly disregarded, since the impact of U.S. aid on the receiving countries and the attitude of the government and people concerned must be the main consideration.

Capital for economic development can be saved, borrowed, stolen, or received as a gift. The most acceptable way for one country to secure technical and economic help from another is to pay for it from domestic savings or foreign loans in the open market. This is the way in which the governments of modern Japan and Germany stimulated the development of their economies. Today there is a certain amount of expropriation, especially by former colonies, and a rising level of expectation among the newer states of receiving capital as a gift from the industrially advanced countries. It is these countries that now have a world platform in the U.N. and are disposed to see that body as a political instrument which can be used to their advantage.

Quaison-Sackey, the Permanent Representative of Ghana to the United Nations, who became President of the General Assembly in 1964, in his book *Africa Unbound,* stresses the anti-colonialism role of the United Nations and the role of the newly freed African nations in the organization. He holds that the quest for international peace is "to be attained by international cooperation in the economic, social, and cultural fields." [24] There has certainly been a "growing tendency to insist on African solutions to African problems, with Africans regarding the U.N. as a vehicle for the purpose." [25] It is clear that the new states of Africa and Asia intend to use

---

[21] Barry Goldwater, quoted in Leonard Freedman and Cornelius P. Cotter (eds.), *Issues of the Sixties* (Belmont, Calif.: Wadsworth Publishing Co., 1961), pp. 385-86.
[22] Quoted in *ibid.,* p. 391.
[23] *Ibid.,* p. 392.
[24] Alex Quaison-Sackey, *Africa Unbound* (New York: Praeger, 1963), p. 125.
[25] Walter Goldschmidt (ed.), *The United States and Africa* (New York: Praeger, 1963), p. 79.

the U.N. not only for political advantage but also for the solution of their economic needs. This has posed a serious problem for the United States. The new states use the U.N. to embarrass the U.S. over the issue of colonial independence movements, possibly in order to induce the U.S. to purchase their good will with economic aid. The political dilemma has been well expressed by William G. Carleton in his *The Revolution in American Foreign Policy:*

> The United States had a difficult time trying to make the new nations realize that while it sympathized with the national aspirations of the colonial peoples it could not afford to alienate its European allies. Indeed, the United States had a difficult time steering a course between the interests of its European allies and the aspirations of the colonial peoples, and the middle position it often pursued only resulted in irritating both. [26]

The abstention of the United States in the General Assembly vote on anti-colonialism was inevitably exploited in the colonial areas to question the true nature of U.S. intentions. Some efforts were made to compensate for this during the Kennedy Administration when the U.S. Government began talking about "Africa for the Africans," took a definite stand against Portuguese policies in Angola, and voted to condemn South Africa's administration of the trust territory of South-West Africa. But the fact of independence has not solved the highly emotional relations between the former colonial areas and their former rulers, and "Time and again, the depth of feeling of both colonial and anti-colonial delegates has affected U.N. discussions even on technical and procedural questions." [27]

These political pressures, combined with the enormous increase in the number of African and Asian members of the United Nations (from 3 to 36 for Africa and from 7 to 20 for Asia) have resulted in a proliferation of United States and U.N. economic activities in these areas. That current U.S. policy favors an increased role for the United Nations in the field of economic aid was indicated by the U.S. Assistant Secretary for International Organization Affairs, Harlan Cleveland:

> The aid programs of the United Nations and other international organizations are also moving rapidly toward a higher level of coordination and effectiveness. The multilateral programs offer a new frontier of foreign aid . . . we know that strengthening the United Nations' capacity

---

[26] William G. Carleton, *The Revolution in American Foreign Policy* (New York: Random House, 1963), pp. 291-92.

[27] Goldschmidt, *op. cit.,* p. 79.

to act on economic and social problems inevitably adds to its capacity to act for peace and security.[28]

The pressure to emphasize multilateral U.N. programs in order to escape the charges of colonialism or political interference is all the stronger, as the Afro-Asian states well know, because the Soviet Union, which actually contributes very little to U.N.-sponsored economic assistance, exploits its propaganda advantages to the full. Generally the Soviet Union has not participated in multilateral economic assistance or development programs. Three main reasons have been given for the Soviet attitude: first, such programs dilute consideration of the major topic, the quest for international peace and security; second, these programs are too "capitalistic-oriented"; and third, since there is no veto in any of the agencies concerned, the Soviet Union cannot prevent action it does not approve. [29] The Soviet Union has joined a few of the purely technical organizations, such as the Universal Postal Union and the World Meteorological Organization, but has refused to participate in those commissions or agencies which have a political context. Since Stalin's death, there has been a slight increase in the U.S.S.R.'s participation in the U.N. aid programs, but this has been minimal. In contrast to the U.S., which gives 40 percent of the cost of the Expanded Program of Technical Assistance and the Special Fund, the Soviet Union has contributed about 3 percent,[30] in unconvertible rubles. Soviet concentration has been on bilateral agreements both inside and outside the Communist bloc. There has recently been some increase in non-bloc assistance, which reflects the changed political situation of the world, particularly in Africa and Asia. The Soviet aid to India and Cuba has been well publicized, as has its support to Egypt's Aswan Dam project. Soviet aid to Africa has grown from $3 million in 1959 to $236 million in 1962; the U.S. total for 1962 exceeds $500 million. The Soviet Union has also made loans or credits available to some African countries including Egypt ($275 million), Ethiopia ($100 million), Libya ($28 million), Guinea ($35 million), Ghana ($40 million), Congo ($3.7 million), Sudan ($22 million), Tunisia ($28 million).[31] Not all of the promised aid arrives, and some of the goods are of poor quality. This selective Soviet economic assistance is seemingly designed to achieve maximum political influence for cold war purposes.

The political case for maintaining U.S. investment in U.N.-sponsored multilateral aid arises out of conditions which are not likely to change and have

---

[28] See *U.S. Participation in the U.N., op. cit.,* p. 171.
[29] Dallin, *op. cit.,* pp. 61-62.
[30] *Ibid.,* p. 68.
[31] Goldschmidt, *op. cit.,* p. 90.

therefore to be taken into account. It can also be argued that the U.S., by increasing the pace of multilateral aid, would have an additional means of building the political and economic foundations of a free market among the countries outside the Communist bloc and of putting pressure on the bloc. There is some debate on whether U.N.-sponsored aid can be used to help to maintain acceptable conditions for private investment and unrestricted international trade, even if it is given with these purposes in mind. It is argued that in practice the aid goes to strengthen the government sector, to weaken private enterprise, and to foster a move toward socialism, thus working against and not for our objectives. [32] Many of these states are already socialist, however, and are likely to remain so for some time. So long as they are not under Communist political control, it is to our political advantage to work with them. It is to our interest to strengthen the economic bonds between the U.S. and the Afro-Asian states, among others, in order to sharpen the contrast between the two major political and economic systems in the world today and to make it more difficult for the Communist powers to disrupt what they cannot control. We should neglect no opportunity to use the U.N. for the promotion of the economic philosophies and institutions of the U.S. and its allies.

Cultural and Humanitarian Functions

Obligations under the Charter

The Charter did not include detailed provisions regarding human rights. While leaving the definition of terms to be one of the early tasks of the Organization, it clearly affirms the faith of the membership in human rights and imposes an obligation on each to honor them; the General Assembly and the Economic and Social Council are empowered to initiate studies and to make recommendations to assist "in the realization of human rights and fundamental freedoms for all without distinction as to race, sex, language, or religion."

The promotion of human rights was nothing new to the U.S., and President Roosevelt on several occasions during the war stressed the need to guarantee these rights to all men. The four freedoms—freedom from want, freedom from fear, freedom of speech and expression, and freedom of worship—were recognized as war aims in the Declaration of the United

---

[32] See P. T. Bauer, *United States Aid and Indian Economic Development* (Washingington, D.C.: American Enterprise Institute, 1959); Milton Friedman, "Foreign Economic Aid: Means and Objectives," *The Yale Review,* Summer 1958; James W. Wiggins and Helmut Schoeck, *Foreign Aid Reexamined* (Washington, D.C.: Public Affairs Press, 1958).

Nations of January 1, 1942. The American view was summarized by the Secretary of State in his report to the President on the results of the San Francisco Conference:

Finally, no sure foundation of lasting peace and security can be laid which does not rest on the voluntary association of free peoples. Only so far as the rights and dignity of all men are respected and protected, only so far as men have free access to information, assurance of free speech and free assembly, freedom from discrimination on grounds of race, sex, language, or religion and other fundamental rights and freedoms, will men insist upon the right to live at peace, to compose such differences as they may have by peaceful methods, and to be guided by reason and good will rather than driven by prejudice and resentment. [33]

In the field of human rights the U.S. has favored a general statement of goals and aspirations rather than a firm set of rules and treaty obligations. The Universal Declaration on Human Rights, adopted by the U.N. on December 10, 1948, deals with civil, political, and economic rights. This declaration is not a treaty and does not impose legally binding commitments on the members. The United States approved of this approach to the problem. As Leland Goodrich suggests, "this position was in part due to reluctance to embark upon the treaty process because of the requirement of Senate approval." [34] The declaration, therefore, depends primarily upon the goodwill of its members and world public opinion for any effectiveness it might have. The U.N. Commission on Human Rights has since tried to draft two Covenants—one on Civil and Political Rights and the other on Economic, Social and Cultural Rights—but these efforts have been abortive largely because of U.S. opposition to entering into any treaty on this subject.

The Draft Conventions

To avoid the controversial ratification question which would be necessary before an all-inclusive treaty or covenant could come into force, the United Nations has resorted to the use of conventions which cover single topics only. These specialized conventions are approved by the General Assembly and submitted to the members for ratification in accordance with their constitutional provisions. Until they are ratified by a member, they have no binding effect within that member's territory even though they may have

---

[33] *Charter of the United Nations,* Report to the President on the Results of the San Francisco Conference by . . . The Secretary of State. Department of State Publication 2349, June 26, 1945, p. 116.
[34] Goodrich, *op. cit.,* p. 248.

been ratified by a majority of members and thus are accepted as general rules of international law. Some American critics of the U.N. consider that these conventions show the sinister nature of the U.N.:

> By the use of the trick word *convention,* they have organized something which is in no sense a convention for the purpose of drawing up international rulings, which, if enforced upon us, would completely destroy our national and state sovereignty. By this tricky, treasonable scheme they would be able to arrest our citizens, try them in foreign courts and sentence them to foreign prisons. [35]

This view ignores the fact that even if the United States Senate should ratify these conventions, enforcement action remains solely in the hands of U.S. officials and agencies. There is still sufficient opposition, on more rational grounds, among the members of the U.S. Senate to prevent ratification of any of the various conventions approved by the majority of the General Assembly.

Much of the reluctance of the U.S. Senate even to consider ratification of several conventions submitted to it arises from the nature of the U.S. federal structure. Opponents of ratification argue that the national government may only commit the states in those matters clearly within the scope of federal power and that for these conventions to be genuinely effective in the U.S., affirmative action by all 50 states would be required. The 1964 Federal Civil Rights Act seems to contradict this argument, but the argument has been effective in preventing serious consideration and ratification by the Senate of the following conventions approved by the Assembly:

1. The Convention Against Genocide was signed by the U.S. but has been pending before the Senate since 1949.

2. The Convention on the Right of Maintenance Abroad (designed to help wives obtain payment from husbands who have fled to other countries) has been pending since 1954.

3. The Convention on the Nationality of Women, adopted in 1954, has not been ratified by the U.S. The U.S., however, is a party to an Inter-American Convention which contains similar provisions.

4. A Supplementary Convention on Abolition of Slavery, passed in 1956, has not been signed or ratified by the U.S., although it was a party to the original convention in 1926.

---

[35] The view of the "Citizens Congressional Committee to Abolish the United Nations," quoted in *The United Nations: The Continuing Debate,* ed. Charles A. Mc-Clelland (San Francisco: Chandler Publishing Co., 1960), p. 15.

5. The ILO Convention on Abolition of Forced Labor, approved in 1957, has not been signed by the U.S.

6. The ILO Convention on the Elimination of Discrimination in Employment has not been ratified by the U.S.

7. The Convention on the Political Rights of Women, approved in 1953, has not been signed by the U.S.

8. The Convention on Protection of Refugees has not been ratified.

9. The UNESCO Convention on Discrimination and Education has not been acted upon by the U.S.

10. The Convention on Marriage Standards entitled "Right to Freedom of Consent in Marriage, Minimum Age in Marriage," has been signed by the U.S.—the first such signature since 1948—but it has not been considered by the U.S. Senate for ratification.

U.S. Presidents since Mr. Truman have varied in their approach to the U.N. conventions. President Truman urged the Senate to approve the Convention on Genocide. The Eisenhower Administration, though it submitted some of these conventions for approval, apparently felt the objectives could be achieved by other means. The Kennedy Administration urged the Senate to ratify the Supplemental Convention on the Abolition of Slavery, the Convention on the Abolition of Forced Labor, and the Convention on the Political Rights of Women. President Kennedy, in his letter of transmittal to the Senate, pointed out that approval would not necessitate any change in domestic legislation, since laws were already in effect in the U.S. which contained the essential points in these conventions. He drew particular attention to the political consequences of failure to approve:

> The fact that our Constitution already assures us of these rights does not entitle us to stand aloof from documents which project our own heritage on an international scale. The day-to-day unfolding of events makes it even clearer that our own welfare is interrelated with the rights and freedoms assured the peoples of other nations.
>
> The conventions deal with human rights which may not yet be secure in other countries; they have provided models for the drafters of constitutions and laws in newly independent nations; and they have influenced the policies of governments preparing to accede to them. Thus, they involve current problems in many countries.
>
> They will stand as a sharp reminder of world opinions to all who may seek to violate the human rights they define. They also serve as a

continuous commitment to respect these rights. There is no society so advanced that it no longer needs periodic recommitment to human rights.

The United States cannot afford to renounce responsibility for support of the very fundamentals which distinguish our concept of government from all *forms of tyranny.*[36]

The conventions concern an area of human endeavor in which the United States and its main allies have unquestioned leadership. The problem is how to exercise it. It would be foolish for the Senate to ratify conventions that would give to other powers, acting through the U.N. Organization, opportunities to urge the U.S. to enforce standards they have no intention of upholding themselves. The safeguards against this happening, however, seem to be sufficient. More serious, perhaps, is the fact that it would be self-defeating to ratify conventions which we have no prospect of enforcing within our own jurisdiction. With these cautions in mind, however, there is still one overwhelming reason why the U.S. should do everything possible to dominate the field of human rights. This relates to the semantic struggle that is being fought in the U.N. as in other fronts in the cold war. It is very important for us for international discourse to be conducted in the language of the Western world, and human rights has to do with some of the most powerful symbols known to man. We are in a better position than anyone else to match the deed to the word and therefore have little excuse to let the battle go by default to the opposition.

---

[36] *U.S. Participation in the U.N., op. cit.,* pp. 241-42.

VII.

UNITED STATES POLICY

The United States and the Soviet Union

Some of the founders of the U.N. thought of it as an exclusive club which would eventually include all states that met the qualifications for membership as they were spelled out in the Charter. The founders publicly committed themselves to the pursuit of certain aims and objectives which were also spelled out in the Charter. We have seen that during the last two decades the rules for membership have been ignored, and the founding fathers have themselves violated the commitments they made to the Organization. A strong tendency towards universality of membership, beginning with the package deals of 1955, has led to the admission of states of almost primitive tribal organization lacking any real sense of responsibility to the international community, [1] of Soviet satellites, and of states with whom the United States has no diplomatic relations. There is nothing exclusive about U.N. membership any more, except that the U.N. has so far successfully resisted the representation of Communist China on the grounds that the Communist regime does not qualify under Article 4 of the Charter. The U.N. has maintained its standards in this one case and lowered them in practically all others, thus bringing about dismay and confusion about its role and purposes.

The attrition of the original concept has been mainly, but not entirely, the

[1] John Paton Davies, *Foreign and Other Affairs* (New York: Norton, 1964), p. 87.

90

work of the Soviet Union. The Soviet Union has almost succeeded in turning the U.N. into a forum which it can use to undermine the prestige and frustrate the policies of the U.S.[2] The Soviet Union has at least been consistent. At no time did it accept the view that the U.N. was an association of states with common purposes. We have been only partially successful in preventing the Soviet Union from destroying what it cannot control or dominating the U.N. for its own exclusive purposes. When the General Assembly adjourned in January 1965, its authority was reduced to its lowest point since 1950 because of the manner in which it reacted to the Soviet-French refusal to contribute to peace-keeping operations. The Secretary-General's office, which depends on the General Assembly for authority, was cut down to size and power was returned to the powerless Security Council. The vast increase in membership that began with the package deals of 1955 has now had its effect on the General Assembly by destroying its morale. This was because so many of the new members are lacking in the attributes of the nation and even, in some cases, of the state. The world has to wait for the states that need the U.N. the most to acquire the political experience and insight to support those policies that will give them protection and save them from further exploitation. For the time being the U.S. lost the initiative in the Assembly and therefore in the U.N.

One thing is quite clear; neither of the great powers is anxious to leave. The Soviets would be reluctant to leave an organization which, without them, might well become an alliance which would be directed against them. On the other hand, the United States would hardly wish, by withdrawing, to turn over the U.N. to the leadership of the Soviet Union. The question for both is what happens to the continuing organization? As Ernest Gross has pointed out:

> Those in our own country who may be led by fear or frustration to urge American withdrawal from the United Nations should likewise ponder the risk that such action on our part might not relinquish leadership, but indeed transfer it to the enemies of freedom.[3]

The dangers of withdrawal are apparently too great for either of the two superpowers to contemplate.

Soviet participation in the U.N. continues, in some measure, because of the current balance of nuclear forces. It is generally agreed that the two superpowers have the capacity to do sufficient damage to each other to make

---
[2] *International Affairs,* "U.N. Rostrum, Forum, Arena," No. 11, November 1963 (Moscow), p. 11.
[3] Gross, *op. cit.,* p. 4.

all-out nuclear war something that both wish to avoid. So long as the current situation remains constant, this analysis is correct, but it is always well to remember that history provides no encouragement for the view that the balance of military power, however horrible and destructive, remains stable. Given a technological advantage in military affairs, the Soviet Union could be expected to use it, not by offering a Baruch-type plan to the world but rather a choice between surrender or destruction.

The development of the U.N. depends a great deal on the bomb. When we had it and the Soviet Union did not, it was to the Kremlin's advantage to stay with the U.N. while building up their military capacity and constantly probing in order to test our intentions. If the Soviet Union had wished to get out of the U.N., it could have done so at the time of the Korean conflict with good reason, from its point of view. But it cannot control or destroy the U.N. until it has military parity or superiority. As Soviet military forces have approached parity, the Soviet Union has demanded more and more a position of equality with the whole of the Western world even in such matters as the number of Soviet officials in all the U.N. organs. The Soviet leaders put the matter in their own way:

> Everyone knows that the preparedness of the Soviet armed forces and the Soviet Union's possibilities of beating back any aggressor are now not in any way unequal to the capability of the imperialist countries to strike first. All Western leaders who take a more or less sober view of the situation now realize this, as otherwise they would not have declared an equal interest in averting a military catastrophe. That is why they have to voice—always with an effort and often inconsistently—their acceptance of co-existence, as President Kennedy did recently.[4]

All this indicates that the Soviet Union realizes that the United Nations Organization is of importance to Soviet foreign policy and that, rather than playing a delaying action as they did for so many years, they are now ready to engage in a real struggle for control. After disposing of the "world government" ideas of many Western jurists and others, a Soviet commentator concludes that "the way out lies not in the replacement of the U.N. by a 'world parliament' or 'world government,' so widely acclaimed in the U.S.A., but in persistent efforts—with the participation of the United Nations too—to solve urgent international problems and thus create favorable conditions for general and complete disarmament and for lasting world peace."[5]

---

[4] *International Affairs*, "Soviet Defense Might and Peaceful Co-Existence," No. 11, November 1963 (Moscow), p. 28.

[5] *International Affairs*, "World Government," No. 12, December 1963 (Moscow), pp. 102-03.

Others have listed *ad nauseam* the ways in which the Soviet Union has broken its pledges to the United Nations as well as to other countries, and the support it has given to others, including Communist China, who have committed aggression or acted in an utterly hostile manner. The argument has been advanced by Alexander Dallin in his comprehensive study of the Soviet Union and the United Nations, that:

> . . . The future of the United Nations is in Soviet hands. Moscow can wreck it or build it up: in the U.N.'s present state, Moscow is unlikely to do either. . . . That bridge between standing international conference and organized international community, which he [Dag Hammarskjold] saw embodied in the U.N. Charter, is certain to remain unfinished so long as Moscow has the right and the might to interpose its veto.[6]

Here is the rub. The Soviet Union undoubtedly has the right to impose its veto, but we know what would happen if it had the might, as a result of a shift in the balance of military power, to impose its will. The effectiveness of U.S. policies towards the United Nations, it is clear, depends in the first and the last instance upon the military might of the United States and its allies.

There is much talk of a dichotomy between support of the United Nations and a dynamic U.S. foreign policy. It is a false dichotomy. Obviously the United Nations is no substitute for a U.S. policy whether dynamic or not; it is both an instrument and an objective of U.S. policy. It is a tool that can be used only for certain purposes; it has its limitations. The United States is a powerful member of the United Nations but is only one power, and the pursuit of policy depends upon the attitudes and policies of other powers, friends as well as foes. The extent to which responsibilities can be accepted by the United Nations and carried out by that body obviously depends upon others as well as ourselves. It would be as reckless to ask the United Nations to handle problems for which it is not set up or not willing to undertake as it would be not to support it in doing those things which it is willing and able to do. We cannot resign from the U.N. and we cannot have a U.N. unless it does something of sufficient significance to stay alive. This is one aspect of the dilemma.

Revision of the Charter?

The framers of the Charter did their work well. Very few of our problems in the United Nations have arisen out of structural defects in its architecture. The remedy for our ills, said Mr. Lester Pearson, who should know, does not lie in changing the Charter but in making it work: "The responsibility for such agreement rests mainly on those members of the United Nations

---

[6] Dallin, *op. cit.*, p. 210.

which have the greatest power and the special privileges." [7] This, however, has not prevented many learned writers from exploring *in vacuo* the benefits that would flow from revision of the Charter. Most of these writers are testing the Charter against an ideal world government with all the attributes of a sovereign state, and their recommendations have little immediate signifiicance. At the same time, some modest changes may be in order. It is probably now possible to adjust the size and composition of the Security Council and the Economic and Social Council to the facts of the international situation today. The Afro-Asian bloc has suggested an increase in the size of these councils. These steps seem to be necessary in order to give the new nations an opportunity to participate, and also to provide for clear-cut regional representation.

The problem first came up in 1956 when the U.N. had increased from 60 to 80 members in a period of two years, half of the new members coming from Asia and Africa. Resolutions to increase the non-permanent membership of the Security Council and to enlarge the UNESCO were before the U.N. from 1956 to 1960. The Assembly went on record as being generally in favor of these measures, but no specific action to amend the Charter was initiated or taken because the Soviet Union made it clear that it would veto any amendment to the Charter so long as Communist China was not represented in the U.N. Two resolutions to amend the Charter were actually introduced in 1960 in order to test the Soviet position. The motion was to increase the number of non-permanent members of the Security Council from 6 to 8 and the membership of UNESCO from 18 to 24. The resolutions were blocked by the threat of a Soviet veto and the two items were dropped from the agenda. The Afro-Asian nations, however, have continued to press for them. Some of these countries urge the U.S.S.R. to separate the problem of Chinese representation from that of Charter revision on the grounds that they are two entirely separate and distinct issues, others have suggested that the enlargement of UNESCO be taken as a first step before pressing for the Security Council changes.

The United States has gone on record as being in favor of both changes but would prefer to push for one at a time on the grounds that enlargement of UNESCO is far less controversial and might be achieved as the first step. In 1963 the Eighteenth General Assembly approved two proposed amendments to the Charter, one to increase the size of the Security Council from 11 to 15 and the Economic and Social Council from 18 to 27 members. The resolution calling for nine additional seats in UNESCO directed that they

[7] Pearson, *op. cit.*, p. 104.

should be divided as follows: seven from African and Asian states, one from Latin American states, one from Western Europe and other states. The ten non-permanent members of the Security Council were to be selected as follows: five from African and Asian states, one from East European states, two from Latin American states, two from Western Europe and other states. As they carried by more than a two-thirds majority, the resolutions were circulated for ratification; neither can become effective until all five permanent members of the Security Council agree.

On this there seemed to be some change in the attitude of the Soviet Union as a result of an announced change in the attitude of the Chinese Communists, who stated that if enlargement of the councils is necessary for adequate representation of the Asian and African members, then they would support such amendments.[8] As late as December 1963, after the Assembly had acted, the Soviet Ministry for Foreign Affairs asserted that: "Solution to the problem has not actually been found," and called for further consultations which should be directed towards solving the basic problem of Chinese Communist representation.[9] On February 10, 1965, without waiting for a solution to the China problem, the Soviet Union became the first of the Big Five to ratify the amendments. The United States, which abstained from voting on both resolutions on a technicality, is on record, however, as being in favor in principle. In effect, the United States has played for time, hoping that extensive consultation and discussion can take place before action must be taken.

The difficulties of bringing about even a modest revision in the Charter are sufficiently impressive to indicate how hard it will be to undertake the general review of the Charter that is required by Article 109 and has been postponed from 1955 until 1965. There is probably much to gain by supporting the modest proposals for expansion of the Councils, but any effort expended on revision of the Charter as a whole would, as we have said, be a waste of time. The United States has quite correctly gone on record as being prepared to participate in a conference to discuss the Charter when conditions are right, but in the American view, and apparently that of the majority of U.N. members, "an attempt at a broad review of the Charter is more likely to prove destructive than constructive." [10] There is every likelihood that the whole question will again be postponed by the Twentieth General Assembly in 1965.

General de Gaulle proposed in early February 1965 that a conference be

---

[8] See *U.S. Participation in the U.N., op. cit.,* p. 153.
[9] *Ibid.,* pp. 153-54.
[10] *Ibid.,* p. 161.

held in Geneva to consider revision of the U.N. Charter. This conference would be attended by the five permanent members of the Security Council with the exception that de Gaulle would substitute Communist China for the Republic of China. At his press conference, General de Gaulle stated that the General Assembly had usurped the powers of the Security Council and "under the pressure of events in Korea, in Suez, in Hungary, and of the immoderate abuse by the Soviets of their veto, the United Nations let themselves go beyond their nature and their possibilities—they went beyond their charter." The de Gaulle proposals are wholly unrealistic because Communist China is not represented in the Organization and the United States would not attend a Charter revision conference where Peiping represented China. It is unlikely that the smaller powers, jealous of their influence in the General Assembly, would approve any proposed Charter changes conceived to restore Big Five domination of the essential work of the United Nations. Nor would the U.S. attend a conference, not to revise the U.N. Charter, but to initiate a new organization.

Future of the General Assembly

The U.N. members who call for a return to the Charter have in mind a reduction in the influence of the General Assembly. Because they amount to more than one-third of the total membership, the Afro-Asian group of states, when they are in agreement, can control General Assembly decisions. They may not always be able to get what they themselves propose, but they can always block anything that anyone else wants. These are the nations that have the least responsibility for keeping the peace, the least capacity for assisting in the maintenance of peace, and the greatest economic needs of all. They are inevitably more interested in their rights as members of the U.N. than in their duties. Up until recently the United States could count upon a favorable vote in the General Assembly, whereas the Soviet Union could not. However, the Assembly has passed a sufficient number of resolutions with which we do not concur, such as the anti-colonial resolution (where we abstained), to cause us to hesitate about giving any more binding force to the actions of the Assembly than there is now.

However large the majorities, the resolutions, declarations, and conventions of the General Assembly are at present merely recommendations which are binding only if ratified by member states. The world has come to expect the Soviet Union to flaunt the majority decisions of the U.N., but not the United States. It is very likely that the United States will find itself, during the next few years, more and more in the position of having to veto or ignore the will of the Assembly. For now that the Afro-Asian states have control of the General Assembly, they are not likely to vote in favor of measures that would reduce such powers as they can exercise there. No member of the Big Five is happy at the thought of being outvoted in the General Assembly, especially since the U.S.-sponsored Uniting for Peace Resolution of 1950 was passed. This much they have in common. Put very simply, the United States is presented with the question of whether to continue to press in the direction of giving the Assembly a share in the peace-keeping function and if so, on what basis? Is it wise to press for changes which would get away from the "one nation, one vote" concept by weighting the votes of those countries upon whose military and economic resources the success of the United Nations depends? Or is this merely another way of returning to the Charter? On the face of it there is no easy way of working out a rational voting pattern in the General Assembly, composed as it is of the rich and the poor, the primitive and the mature, the weak and the strong, old empires and former colonies, among whom there is no common value system, no agreed-upon goals. At the present time there is no basis here for a parliament of man.

Does this mean, however, that the General Assembly, even under present rules and conditions is an arena from which the U.S. needs to run away? Is not the United States in a much better position than the Soviet Union to win the sympathy and the votes of the underdeveloped states. It is important to realize that we do not need the votes of any Communist state in order to get things done in the General Assembly. If the United States can keep the initiative in the Assembly by dominating the field of economic and technical assistance, the general interests of U.S. policy can be well served. It is definitely to our interest to see to it that new nations remain not only peaceful but viable.

The General Assembly as presently constituted must again be made into a useful instrument for U.S. policies, both political and economic, in spite of its obvious shortcomings. There is more to be gained by returning to the Assembly the power it had acquired than in returning to the Charter, as the slogan goes, which means clipping the wings of the Assembly. It is too late now to turn the clock back; the primitive states cannot be ejected. The far too rapid disintegration of the empires has taken place and the consequences have to be endured. The United States, as we have seen, has to share the blame for reducing the General Assembly to impotence and so helping to destroy an instrument of great political flexibility. It is going to take time for the new states to gain experience, but in the long run there is more to be gained by using the new states to redress the balance of the old than by associating ourselves with big-power domination of the Security

Council, in which some of the main enemies of the U.N. have the veto. Another consideration is that failure to rebuild the prestige and authority of the Assembly will encourage the smaller powers to look favorably on possible rival institutions to the United Nations. We have to turn the present weakness of the Assembly into future strength. One way to do this would be to revise the procedure of the General Assembly, putting the peace-keeping functions, for example, in the hands of a responsible committee, as the U.S. has already suggested. We have to gain time while our long-range policies of general economic and technical assistance to the new states take effect. It is essential to keep the initiative in the Assembly in order to force the Communists to fight the battle of coexistence on our terms instead of theirs. This is another way of saying that the long-range objective of the U.S. must be to lay the foundations among the non-Communist states of a common purpose, common values, and common commitments.

United States Strategy and Tactics

The Charter of the U.N. was drawn up in the hope that big-power cooperation would lead to a general consensus for peace; today there is no consensus, no big-power cooperation, and little respect for the Charter. The history of the U.N. has been one of relentless efforts on the part of the Soviet Union within, and Communist China without, to undermine its effectiveness. Twenty years of history have been dominated almost completely by the cold war. The world has come to accept the fact that the Communist powers have no sympathy whatsoever with U.S. efforts to achieve a consensus on the basis of cultural and political pluralism. If the U.N. has not produced the consensus hoped for, this has been largely, but not entirely due to the fact that it has been the battleground for one of the greatest divisions in world history. In fact, the modest degree of cooperation given to the U.N. by the U.S. and its allies derives in large measure from reactions to the Communist challenge.

There are those who think it would be better for the U.S. to accept the fact that the U.N. has failed, give up any hope for its future, let it die and while it is dying, use it for our own short-range national interests. According to this view, the U.N. has reached a dead end, it is a mockery of American hopes and ideals, and so long as the Communist powers are members it can never succeed. The U.N., runs the argument, was born out of American reforming zeal and is supported only by do-gooders; it has gone the way of the earlier efforts such as Prohibition, to legislate goodness. These views are not without foundation but the conclusion does not follow from the argument. It is not our decision alone as to whether or not the U.N. shall survive or as to what would happen if we assumed the role of pallbearer. The U.N.

has deep roots and is far too valuable a political symbol, particularly to the Afro-Asian states, to be buried, especially by its originator.

The chief reason why these views are irrelevant is that every nation which is threatened by nuclear destruction has a vital interest in maintaining an organization which is strong enough to help control that threat. The U.S., therefore, could hardly take the initiative in destroying the U.N. unless it had something to put in its place. As we do not, our political and psychological investment is still worth protecting. The U.N. has a real appeal to the middle and small powers who cannot protect themselves, and it would be poor politics to forfeit their interest. They are the main contributors to the U.N.'s modest but significant efforts to control the sort of brush fires that might otherwise lead to all-out war. In a world that tends to be organized more and more along supra-national lines the U.N. can serve as an arbiter and adjuster.

Although most of the power conflicts go on outside the U.N., there are occasions on which the U.N. machinery can be used to common advantage. It is not that the U.N. itself resolves the issues; it can be used for gaining time, lowering tensions, and saving face. The settlement of the Berlin blockade is often given as an example of this function of the U.N. Rightly or wrongly, it was possible for the British and French to stop their operations in the Suez in the name of the U.N., and although the U.N. did nothing to prevent the Soviet intervention in Hungary, at least the Soviet action was well advertised to the world by means of a highly critical U.N. report.

The U.N. is politically important because it is based upon Western legal, political, and economic ideas. It stems from the Western intellectual tradition; it owes something to the experience of the League of Nations. The Western world has produced the only set of concepts and institutions that provide any hope for the development of a peaceful world. It is difficult to overrate the importance for the U.S. of maintaining the initiative in the international discourse concerning methods of achieving world peace or of compelling the Communists to discuss these matters in our terms, not theirs. It is very much to the interest of the U.S. that a future international organization for peace, whatever shape it might take, should grow out of the present U.N.

The financial cost of the U.N. to the U.S. is not high. Our share of the total annual cost, of which we pay 32 percent, amounted in 1964 to $29,-411,000; contributions to UNEF and UNOC came to $15,700,000; voluntary payments to such things as UNICEF, EPTA, and the U.N. High Commissioner for Palestine Refugees amounted to $52,000,000. Of the $200,000,-000 bond issue the U.S. has bought around $75,500,000. This is well within our means. We have given up no part of our sovereignty; no other powers can bind us through the U.N. to do anything to which we do not agree. On the other hand, in a war which we decided to fight for our own national interest, the Korean War, we had the assistance of 16 nations and the moral advantage of having the General Assembly denounce the enemy as an aggressor. The U.S. has had from the U.N. a rich return for its investment, not least among the returns being the political asset of sponsoring an organization for peace.

The long-range policy of the U.S. has to be based on the assumption that the U.N. can be an effective guarantor of the peace only when there is a consensus of the major powers to which the Communists are the main, if not the only, obstacle. Even in theory they are not in favor of coexistence in our sense of the term; Communist ideas of national and international organization simply do not fit in with our ideas of international relations. As only the future can decide whether or not they will change, the present course for U.S. policy is clear. It is to cultivate a consensus—based on as large a measure as possible of moral, political, and economic homogeneity— among those states that have no commitment to the Communist powers. Put in practical terms, consensus includes a willingness to use means short of war to bring about social change or to resolve international conflicts; a significant degree of agreement, therefore, on moral values; and commitment to common standards of legal, political, and economic relations. These objectives must be pursued within the framework of the existing U.N., which presents some difficulties, but it is doubtful whether that task would be any easier if we could make a clean start without the Communist powers. We have seen how Communist intransigeance has helped to consolidate the Western alliances and *détente* tends to disintegrate them. The only course for U.S. policy is a pragmatic, instrumental approach to the U.N. While retaining the initiative in bringing about growth and change we have to give the achievement of the consensus first priority, for this is the basis for an effective future U.N. as well as for the ultimate resolution of our differences with the Communist world. The task of statesmanship is to use the U.N. as it is today as one of the means by which to solidify the non-Communist powers for common purposes.

There are two main approaches to bringing about this long-range objective. One is political, the other economic. Politically, the task of building a consensus has to be done in such a way as not to create more problems in the U.N. than can be handled at any given time. It should be our policy to insist as far as possible upon observance of the rules of the U.N. as embodied in the Charter, not however to the point of destroying the institution.

It should be done in such a way as to secure the cooperation of our allies, not merely to expose the opposition. We have to continue to give high priority to the maintenance of such alliances as NATO and SEATO, the multilateral arrangements with Latin America, and bilateral security agreements with such countries as Japan. It is in these regional arrangements that we are working out the ticklish problem of the relation between national sovereignty and international organization, which, as Hans Morgenthau reminds us, is the key problem.[11] The political task of achieving a consensus begins, indeed, with our closest and most powerful allies. We cannot go any faster than they will permit. For example, the purist would insist that all members fulfill their financial responsibilities to the U.N. and that those who vote for action involving the use of military force should make their appropriate contributions to its cost. In the application of policy, however, it may be justifiable at times to retreat on one issue in order to gain time on another so long as the general direction of policy is firmly set on course. The fact that France took the same position as the Soviet Union on the financial question was in itself sufficient cause for caution in choosing the time and place in which to resolve the matter. It is wiser to reach a solution with France first and have France on our side. If this can be done the time purchased by postponement of the Nineteenth General Assembly will have been a good investment, however high the cost to our prestige.

In the long run it might be better to put the peace-keeping function on a basis of voluntary contributions in order to keep the principle alive than to paralyze the U.N. completely by insisting on a literal interpretation of Article 19 of the Charter. At this stage there is much to be said for the idea that those who do not wish to contribute can abstain and those who do can go ahead irrespective of the views of the non-contributors.

The Nineteenth General Assembly adjourned in order to give a new committee time to report, by June 15, 1965, on all aspects of the peace-keeping operations. The Secretary-General identified the problem in his speech of February 20 as one of whether peace-keeping should be shared between the Security Council and the General Assembly or left entirely to the great powers, as France and the Soviet Union propose. In view of the record no supporter of the U.N. would advocate a return to the Charter. In September 1964, the United States suggested that the Assembly should take over if the Security Council failed to act, but only on the advice of a committee dominated by those countries which contributed most heavily to the practical task

---

[11] Hans J. Morgenthau, "The U.N. of Dag Hammarskjold Is Dead," *New York Times Magazine*, March 14, 1965, p. 32.

of peace-keeping. A solution along these lines would avoid giving the reins to the Assembly as presently constituted and would further U.S. policies by permitting the peace-keeping function to develop. It is entirely in keeping with the spirit of the Charter that contributions to peace-keeping should be voluntary. As the London *Economist* put it,

> . . . if reluctant powers are not required either to pay for an operation or to vote formally in support of it, they can often tacitly accept and let it go forward. The value of this kind of silent consent may be the most important discovery made during the new "great debate." [12]

The China representation issue, almost as old as the U.N., raises very difficult problems with our allies if we are to give priority to achieving a consensus. The British, the French, and possibly the Japanese, favor seating Communist China. Their position differs from that of the U.S. largely for historical reasons. Unlike the U.S. they are not involved in the unfinished Chinese civil war. As a result of Chinese intervention in Korea, not as a matter of original intent or design, the United States has given economic and military support to Taiwan and is now committed by treaty to the defense of that island against Communist attack. Taiwan is part of the larger defensive position in the western Pacific which is designed to prevent the further expansion of Communist aggression. The seating of Chinese Communist representatives at the U.N. under present conditions would have a negative impact upon the morale of America's allies in that part of the world.

It is true that the Chinese people are represented in the U.N. by a government which has been driven off the mainland by a rival regime and that the vast majority have no one speaking directly for them in the U.N. Nor can it be said that the Peiping regime is any less in tune with the people it controls than are many other regimes now in the U.N. But proportional representation is not the issue because it is not the basis of U.N. membership. The issue is that in addition to its open attacks on the U.N. in Korea, Peiping and Taiwan are engaged in an unresolved civil war. It is because the outcome is still in doubt that Peiping would like to have the civil war settled in its favor by having the U.N. deprive the Nationalists of their international recognition and support. The Chinese Communists accepted Soviet support and protection before and after they came to power but bitterly criticize U.S. support of the Nationalist Government as interference in the civil war. On all other matters the Communists do not favor U.N. intervention, but in this

---

[12] London *Economist*, February 27, 1965, pp. 875-76.

case they call on the U.N., in effect, to help them bring the civil war to a successful conclusion.

The U.S. has found ways of dealing with Peiping that are tolerable if not adequate. The meetings at Warsaw, on the ambassadorial level, probably provide better contact than that enjoyed by several countries that have formal diplomatic relations with Peiping. The recently acquired nuclear status of Peiping raises a more serious matter of communication in view of the argument that no disarmament proposals worthy of the name can be entered into without the cooperation of Communist China and that disarmament is the business of the U.N. This is true, but disarmament is simply not in the realm of practical politics, whereas arms control, the more important issue, is a subject that can be negotiated without recognition or membership in the U.N. The partial test-ban treaty, for example, was concluded outside the U.N. Arms control rests on tacit agreements as well as overt treaties. Thus, while it would certainly be to the interest of the U.S. to include Communist China in arms control measures, this is an entirely different matter from representation in the U.N.

Let us put the China problem in perspective. There are other civil wars in the world today which have been created or intensified by Communist action—two Germanies, Koreas, Vietnams—that are of equal if not greater urgency and magnitude. They also raise problems of representation. The difference is that one of the Chinas has a permanent seat on the Security Council and the other China has, in effect, been at war with the U.N. since 1950. If the civil conflict cannot be resolved, the problem of policy comes down to the question of what sort of international status we are willing to accord to the National Government on Taiwan and the People's Democratic Republic. As the U.S. is not going to open Taiwan to a Communist takeover or assist the Nationalists in returning to the mainland, unless we are at war with Peiping, the status quo is likely to last a long time.

If we have to accept an Assembly vote to seat Peiping, we have at least two alternatives. One would be to insist that Nationalist China remain in the Assembly and urge her to surrender her permanent seat on the Security Council on condition that it would be given to no other power. As Communist China is not a great power it has no more claim to a permanent seat than does Nationalist China. As Nationalist China would have equal status with Communist China in the Assembly, she would not lose any more prestige than she has already. At present Peiping would not accept, but there is no guarantee that she would not accept if the occasion arose. Sooner or later the international status of Nationalist China has to correspond to the facts of power. By giving up the permanent seat on the Security Council, she could deny it to Peiping. This is a bargain that would appeal to many of our allies that wish to bring Peiping into the U.N. but do not wish to throw Nationalist China out. It could turn the tables on Peiping in the General Assembly.

Another course of action would be to fight the issue in the Security Council and accept the disapproval of some of our allies and of the majority in the Assembly. The comparative advantages and disadvantages of each course would depend on circumstances at the time. At present U.S. purposes are best served by keeping Peiping out of the U.N.

The achievement of a political consensus will also depend on the economic policies of the United States. In a general sense it is probably true that the larger the number of states which accept and practice the economic patterns of the Western world, the better the political prospects. The specialized agencies of the U.N. that deal with economic matters are Western in character. They can be used as instruments with which to strengthen and promote our way of doing business. The objective of U.S. policy in this sphere must be to increase international trade and press for an ever-widening open market, to push for free enterprise in every part of the non-Communist world, while accepting the economic pluralism of the Western world and coming to terms with the Common Market. The general direction of policy must be to sharpen the contrast between the two great economic systems and to bring as much of the non-committed world as possible into an interdependent, Western-oriented, economic system. It has been to our advantage that most of the major powers, excepting the Communist bloc, have cooperated in the field of U.N. economic and technical assistance. To surrender U.S. initiative in the economic and related activities of the U.N. and the specialized agencies would be to throw away an extremely valuable asset, a major instrument of U.S. policy.

The problem of how much to implement economic policy through the U.N. and how much through bilateral arrangements has to be solved in a pragmatic fashion. Political considerations will sometimes be as important as economic. A case in point is the role that the U.S. should play in the World Food Program established by resolution of the U.N. The FAO World Food Program is set up to make surplus food available to food-deficient peoples through the United Nations mechanism. According to the FAO report, one-half of the world's population is malnourished or undernourished. This food program is supposedly designed not so much to feed the starving as to help these countries to feed themselves.

The U.S. has to weigh the political gain of cooperating, even if it makes a larger contribution than others, against making its help conditional on the acceptance of similar responsibility by other food-surplus countries which are doing far less than they could. It is self-defeating to take over burdens that should be shared by our allies, but at the same time it would be quixotic to reduce the U.S. contribution in order to prove a point against the U.S.S.R. when so much more can be gained by emphasizing the contrast between the U.S. approach and that of the Soviet Union.

A U.N. is necessary not to replace diplomacy but to make it possible, especially in view of the way in which Communist states practice that ancient art; not to do away with blocs and alliances but to make them manageable; not to bring the millennium but to focus world attention on the inevitable struggles for power and to find institutions within which they can be regulated. There is nothing millennial or redemptionist about U.S. policy in the U.N.; we have received good value for our efforts. The mistakes and failures of U.S. policy have come not as the result of exaggerated idealism or optimism about the U.N. but rather from a failure to understand and identify the hostile intent, the strategy and tactics of the Soviet Union and other Communist powers.

The problem is to strike the right balance, keeping in mind the importance of building a consensus among as many states as possible. Action must be calculated not in terms of a static model of a U.N. which does not in fact exist but rather in terms of a developmental approach. The task is to construct the political, moral, and economic foundations of a future U.N. within the present structure of the old U.N. and in the teeth of strong opposition.

APPENDIX A

The United Nations Membership—April 1, 1965

The General Assembly

The General Assembly is the only principal organ of the United Nations on which all 114 members are represented. These are listed below:

Afghanistan	Greece	Nigeria
Albania	Guatemala	Norway
Algeria	Guinea	Pakistan
Argentina	Haiti	Panama
Australia	Honduras	Paraguay
Austria	Hungary	Peru
Belgium	Iceland	Philippines
Bolivia	India	Poland
Brazil	Iran	Portugal
Bulgaria	Iraq	Rumania
Burma	Ireland	Rwanda
Burundi	Israel	Saudi Arabia
Byelorussian S.S.R.	Italy	Senegal
Cambodia	Ivory Coast	Sierra Leone
Cameroon	Jamaica	Somalia
Canada	Japan	South Africa
Central African Republic	Jordan	Spain
Ceylon	Kenya	Sudan
Chad	Kuwait	Sweden
Chile	Laos	Syrian Arab Republic
China	Lebanon	Tanzia, United Republic of
Colombia	Liberia	Thailand
Congo (Brazzaville)	Libya	Togo
Congo (Leopoldville)	Luxembourg	Trinidad and Tobago
Costa Rica	Madagascar	Tunisia
Cuba	Malawi	Turkey
Cyprus	Malaysia	Uganda
Czechoslovakia	Mali	Ukrainian S.S.R.
Dahomey	Malta	U.S.S.R.
Denmark	Mauritania	United Arab Republic
Dominican Republic	Mexico	United Kingdom
Ecuador	Mongolia	United States
El Salvador	Morocco	Upper Volta
Ethiopia	Nepal	Uruguay
Finland	Netherlands	Venezuela
France	New Zealand	Yemen
Gabon	Nicaragua	Yugoslavia
Ghana	Niger	Zambia

APPENDIX B

Excerpts from General Assembly recommendations to Security Council, recommendations to permanent members, November 2, 1950; Resolution A, Uniting for Peace:

Recalling its resolution 290 (IV) entitled "Essentials of Peace," which states that disregard of the Principles of the Charter of the United Nations is primarily responsible for the continuance of international tension, and desiring to contribute further to the objectives of that resolution,

Reaffirming the importance of the exercise by the Security Council of its primary responsibility for the maintenance of international peace and security, and the duty of the permanent members to seek unanimity and to exercise restraint in the use of the veto,

*   *   *   *   *   *   *   *   *

Conscious that failure of the Security Council to discharge its responsibilities on behalf of all the Member states, particularly those responsibilities referred to in the two preceding paragraphs, does not relieve Member states of their obligations or the United Nations of its responsibility under the Charter to maintain international peace and security,

Recognizing in particular that such failure does not deprive the General Assembly of its rights or relieve it of its responsibilities under the Charter in regard to the maintenance of international peace and security,

Recognizing that discharge by the General Assembly of its responsibilities in these respects calls for possibilities of observation which would ascertain the facts and expose aggressors; for the existence of armed forces which could be used collectively; and for the possibility of timely recommendation by the General Assembly to Members of the United Nations for collective action which, to be effective, should be prompt,

Resolves that if the Security Council, because of lack of unanimity of the permanent members, fails to exercise its primary responsibility for the maintenance of international peace and security in any case where there appears to be a threat to the peace, breach of the peace, or act of aggression, the General Assembly shall consider the matter immediately with a view to making appropriate recommendations to Members for collective measures, including in the case of a breach of the peace or act of aggression the use of armed force when necessary, to maintain or restore international peace and security. If not in session at the time, the General Assembly may meet in emergency special session within 24 hours of the request therefor. Such emergency special session shall be called if requested by the Security Council on the vote of any seven members, or by a majority of the Members of the United Nations;

*   *   *   *   *   *   *   *   *

Invites each Member of the United Nations to survey its resources in order to determine the nature and scope of the assistance it may be in a position to render in support of any recommendations of the Security Council or of the General Assembly for the restoration of international peace and security;

Recommends to the states Members of the United Nations that each Member maintain within its national armed forces elements so trained, organized, and equipped that they could promptly be made available, in accordance with its constitutional processes, for service as a United Nations unit or units, upon recommendation by the Security Council or General Assembly, without prejudice to the use of such elements in exercise of the right of individual or collective self-defence recognized in Article 51 of the Charter;

*   *   *   *   *   *   *   *   *

The General Assembly, in adopting the proposals set forth above, is fully conscious that enduring peace will not be secured solely by collective security arrangements against breaches of international peace and acts of aggression, but that a genuine and lasting peace depends also upon the observance of all the Principles and Purposes established in the Charter of the United Nations, upon the implementation of the resolutions of the Security Council, the General Assembly, and other principal organs of the United Nations intended to achieve the maintenance of international peace and security, and especially upon respect for and observance of human rights and fundamental freedoms for all and on the establishment and maintenance of conditions of economic and social well-being in all countries; and accordingly

Urges Member states to respect fully, and to intensify, joint action, in co-operation with the United Nations, to develop and stimulate universal respect for and observance of human rights and fundamental freedoms, and to intensify individual and collective efforts to achieve conditions of economic stability and social progress, particularly through the development of under-developed countries and areas.

*   *   *   *   *   *   *   *   *

The General Assembly

Recommends to the Security Council:

That it should take the necessary steps to ensure that the action provided for under the Charter is taken with respect to threats to the peace, breaches of the peace, or acts of aggression and with respect to the peaceful settlement of disputes or situations likely to endanger the maintenance of international peace and security;

That it should devise measures for the earliest application of Articles 43, 45, 46, and 47 of the Charter of the United Nations regarding the placing of armed forces at the disposal of the Security Council by the states Members of the United Nations and the effective functioning of the Military Staff Committee.

The above disposition should in no manner prevent the General Assembly from fulfilling its functions under resolution A.

*　*　*　*　*　*　*　*　*

APPENDIX C

General Assembly Votes on Chinese Representation

The votes from 1951 through 1960 are votes *for* a moratorium on the question of which government should represent China in the U.N. In short, these are not "for" and "against" Peiping or Taiwan votes; they postpone the issue.

Session	For	Against	Abstaining	Absent	Total
6 (1951)	37	11	4	8	60
7 (1952)	42	7	11	0	60
8 (1953)	44	10	2	4	60
9 (1954)	43	11	6	0	60
10 (1955)	42	12	6	0	60
11 (1956)	47	24	8	0	79
12 (1957)	48	27	7	0	82
13 (1958)	44	28	9	0	81
14 (1959)	44	29	9	0	82
15 (1960)	42	34	22	1	99

The votes from 1961 through 1963 are on the specific question of allowing the Communist Chinese to have the China seat.

16 (1961)	36	48	20	0	104
17 (1962)	42	56	12	0	110
18 (1963)	41	57	12	0	110
19 (1964)	No vote				

APPENDIX D

Senate Concurrent Resolution 34 *

August 31, 1961

CHINA

Whereas the Government of the United States enjoys close and friendly relations with the Government of the Republic of China, including treaty obligations which this Government honors; and

Whereas the Republic of China has faithfully discharged its obligations under the Charter of the United Nations; and

Whereas the Chinese Communist Government has flagrantly violated basic human rights, has imposed on the Chinese people one of the most brutal regimes known to history, and is without authority to speak for the Chinese people other than the authority that derives from usurpation and tyranny; and

Whereas the Chinese Communist regime by its aggression in Korea, its repression in Tibet, its threats against its neighbors, its failure to release American prisoners as promised, its export of narcotics to non-Communist countries, on a scale that makes it the major source of the international illicit narcotics traffic, and its hostility toward the United States and the United Nations has demonstrated that it is not qualified for representation in the United Nations: Therefore be it

Resolved by the Senate (the House of Representatives concurring), that it is the sense of the Congress that the United States shall continue to meet its commitments to the people and Government of the Republic of China and shall continue to support that Government as the representative of China in the United Nations; and be it further

Resolved, that the United States shall continue to oppose the seating of the Chinese Communist regime in the United Nations so long as that regime persists in defying the principles of the United Nations Charter; and be it further

Resolved, that it is the sense of the Congress that the American people support the President in not according diplomatic recognition to the Chinese Communist regime.

Agreed to August 31, 1961.

* *United States Statutes at Large,* 1961, Vol. 75, pp. 965-66.

BIBLIOGRAPHY

Aims of the United Nations. Introduction by James T. Shotwell, New York: Dutton, 1955

Appleton, Sheldon, *The Eternal Triangle.* East Lansing: Michigan State University Press, 1961

Attlee, Clement R., *The Future of United Nations.* Indian Council for Cultural Relations, New Delhi: Allied Publishers Private Ltd., 1961

Bailey, Sydney D., *The Secretariat of the United Nations.* New York: Carnegie Endowment for International Peace, 1962

Bailey Sydney D., *The United Nations, A Short Political Guide.* New York: Frederick A. Praeger, 1962

Banfield, Edward C., *American Foreign Aid Doctrines.* Washington, D.C.: American Enterprise Institute, 1963

Bauer, P. T., *United States Aid and Indian Economic Development.* Washington, D. C.: American Enterprise Institute, 1959

Black, Joseph E. and Kenneth W. Thompson, *Foreign Policies in a World of Change.* New York: Harper & Row, 1963

Bloomfield, Lincoln P. (ed. by). *International Military Forces.* Boston: Little, Brown & Co., 1964.

Boyd, Andrew, *The United Nations Handbook.* New York: Pilot Press, 1946

Boyd, Andrew, *United Nations: Piety, Myth and Truth.* Baltimore: Penguin Books, 1962

Bullitt, William C., *The Great Globe Itself.* New York: Scribner, 1946

Calvocoressi, Peter, *World Order and New States.* New York: Praeger for The Institute for Strategic Studies, 1962

Carleton, William G., *The Revolution in American Foreign Policy.* New York: Random House, 1963

China and the United Nations. China Institute of International Affairs, New York: Manhattan Publishing Co., 1959

Clark, Grenville and Louis B. Sohn, *World Peace Through World Law.* Cambridge Mass.: Harvard University Press, 1960

Cohen, Benjamin V., *The United Nations: Constitutional Development, Growth and Possibilities.* Cambridge: Harvard University Press, 1961

111

112

Courlander, Harold, *Shaping Our Times—What the United Nations Is and Does.*
New York: Oceana Publications, 1960
Cousin, Norman, *In Place of Folly.* New York: Harper, 1961
Coyle, David Cushman, *The United Nations and How It Works.* New York: Columbia University Press, 1961
Dallin, Alexander, *The Soviet Union at the United Nations.* New York: Praeger, 1962
Davies, John Paton, *Foreign and Other Affairs.* New York: Norton, 1964
Deane, John R., *The Strange Alliance.* New York: The Viking Press, 1947.
Development Through Food. Freedom from Hunger Campaign, Basic Study No. 2, Food and Agricultural Organization. Rome, 1962
Eagleton, Clyde, *The United Nations and the United States.* Dallas: Southern Methodist University, 1951
Ebenstein, William, *Today's ISMS.* Englewood Cliffs, N. J.: Prentice-Hall, 1964
Eichelberger, Clark N., *UN—The First Fifteen Years.* New York: Harper & Brothers, 1960
Evatt, Herbert V., *The United Nations.* Cambridge: Harvard University Press, 1948
Fenichell, Stephen S., *The United Nations: Design for Peace.* New York: Holt, Rinehart and Winston, 1960
The Forrestal Diaries. Walter Millis, ed. New York: Viking Press, 1951.
Freedman, Leonard and Cornelius P. Cotter, *Issues of The Sixties.* Belmont, California: Wadsworth Publishing Co., 1961
Friedman, Milton, "Foreign Economic Aid: Means and Objectives," *The Yale Review,* Summer 1958.
Friedmann, Wolfgang. *The Changing Structure of International Law.* London: Stevens and Sons, 1964
Friedrich, Carl J. and Zbigniew K. Brzezinski, *Totalitarian Dictatorship and Autocracy.* New York: Frederick A. Praeger, 1961
Goldschmidt, Walter, *The United States and Africa.* New York: Frederick A. Praeger, 1963
Goodrich, Leland M., *The United Nations.* New York: Crowell, 1959
Goodwin, Geoffrey L., *Britain and the United Nations.* New York: Manhattan Publishing Co., 1957
Greene, Fred, *Dynamics of International Relations.* New York: Holt, Rinehart & Winston, 1964
Gross, Ernest A., *The United Nations: Structure for Peace.* New York: Council on Foreign Relations by Harper, 1962.
Gunther, John, *Roosevelt in Retrospect.* New York: Harper, 1950
Hadwen, John G., *How United Nations Decisions Are Made.* Leyden: A. W. Sythoff, 1960
Hall, Gordon D., *The Hate Campaign Against the UN.* Boston: Beacon Press, 1952
Hammarskjold, Dag, *The International Civil Service in Law and in Fact.* Oxford: Clarendon Press, 1961
Hammarskjold Forum—Background Papers and Proceedings. Dobbs Ferry, New York: Oceana Publications, 1963
Higgins, Rosalyn, *The Development of International Law Through the Political Organs of the United Nations.* London: Oxford University Press, 1963
Hovet, Thomas, *Africa in the United Nations.* Evanston, Ill.: Northwestern University Press, 1963
Hovet, Thomas, *Bloc Politics in the United Nations.* Cambridge: Harvard University Press, 1960
Hull, Cordell, *The Memoirs of Cordell Hull.* New York: The Macmillan Co., 1948

113

Hunter, Edward, *The Black Book on Red China*. New York: Bookmailer, 1958
India and the United Nations. New York: Manhattan Publishing Co., 1957
International Law in a Changing World. Contributions by C. Wilfred Jenks and others. Dobbs Ferry, New York: Oceana Publications, 1963.
Khrushchev in New York. New York: Crosscurrents Press, 1960
Langrod, Georges, *The International Civil Service*. Leyden: A. W. Sythoff, 1963
Lash, Joseph P., *Dag Hammarskjold; Custodian of the Brushfire Peace*. Garden City, New York: Doubleday, 1961
Leites, Nathan, *A Study of Bolshevism*. Glencoe, Ill.: Free Press, 1953
Lie, Trygve, *In the Cause of Peace*. New York: Macmillan 1954
Mackintosh, J. M., *Strategy and Tactics of Soviet Foreign Policy*. New York: Oxford University Press, 1963
Marshall, Charles Burton, "Conflict and Consensus in the United Nations," in Jeanne J. Kirkpatrick (ed.), *The Strategy of Deception*. New York: Farrar, Straus, 1963
McClelland, Charles A., *The United Nations: The Continuing Debate*. San Francisco: Chandler, 1960
McClure, William M., *World Legal Order*. Chapel Hill: University of North Carolina Press, 1960
Malik, Charles, *Man in the Struggle for Peace*. New York: Harper & Row, 1963
Mendlovitz, Saul H. (edited and compiled by), *Legal and Political Problems of World Order*. New York: The Fund for Education Concerning World Peace Through World Law, 1962
Miller, Richard I., *Dag Hammarskjold and Crisis Diplomacy*, New York: Oceana Publications, 1961
Moore, Raymond A., Jr. (edited with an introduction by), *The United Nations Reconsidered*. Studies in International Affairs No. 2. Institute of International Studies, Columbia, South Carolina: University of South Carolina Press, 1963
Munro, Sir Leslie, *United Nations: Hope for a Divided World*. New York: Holt, 1960
Nicholas, Herbert G., *The United Nations as a Political Institution*. London: Oxford University Press, 1962
Niemeyer, Gerhart with John S. Reshetar, Jr., *An Inquiry Into Soviet Mentality*. New York: Frederick A. Praeger, 1956
Pearson, Lester B., *A Critical Evaluation of the United Nations*. Vancouver: University of British Columbia Press, 1961
Pearson, Lester B., *The Four Faces of Peace*. New York: Dodd, Mead & Co., 1964
Quaison-Sackey, Alex, *Africa Unbound*. New York: Frederick A. Praeger, 1963
Raj, B. V. Govinda, *India and Disputes in the UN 1946-54*. Bombay: Vora, 1959
Revision of the United Nations Charter, A Symposium. Indian Council of World Affairs: New Delhi: Allahbad Law Journal Press, 1956
Russell, Ruth B. and Jeannette E. Muther, *A History of the United Nations Charter*. Washington: The Brookings Institution, 1958
Sharp, Walter R., *Field Administration in the United Nations System*. London: Stevens and Sons Limited, 1961
Sherwood, Robert E., *Roosevelt and Hopkins*. New York: Harper & Brothers, 1948
Sohn, Louis B., *Basic Documents of the United Nations*. Brooklyn: Foundation Press, 1956
Spiro, Herbert J., *Politics in Africa, Prospects South of the Sahara*. Englewood Cliffs, N.J.: Prentice-Hall, 1962
Stevenson, Adlai E., *Looking Outward. Years of Crisis at the United Nations*. New York: Harper & Row, 1963
Stoessinger, John G., *The Might of Nations: World Politics in Our Times*. New York: Random House, 1961

Stone, Julius, *Aggression and World Order. A Critique of United Nations Theories of Aggression.* Berkeley: University of California Press, 1958
The United Nations—Its Record and Its Prospects. New York: Carnegie Endowment for International Peace, 1950
The U. S. Stake in the UN, American Assembly. New York: Graduate School of Business, Columbia University, 1954
Thompson, Kenneth W. *Christian Ethics and the Dilemmas of Foreign Policy.* Durham, N.C.: Duke University Press, 1959
Uhl, Alexander, *The US and The UN, Partners for Peace.* Washington: Public Affairs Institute, 1962
U.S. Participation in the U.N. Report by the President to the Congress for the year 1963, Department of State Publication 7675, International Organization and Conference Series 51, August 1964
Vandenbosch, Amy and Willard N. Hogan, *Toward World Order.* New York: McGraw-Hill, 1963
Van Slyck, Philip, *Peace: The Control of National Power.* Boston: Beacon Press, 1963
Voss, Earl H., *Nuclear Ambush.* Chicago: H. Regnery Co., 1963
Weissberg, Guenther, *The International Status of the United Nations.* New York: Oceana Publications, 1961
Wiggins, James W., and Helmut Schoeck, *Foreign Aid Reexamined.* Washington, D. C.: Public Affairs Press, 1958
Wilcox, Francis O. and H. Field Haviland, Jr. *The United States and the United Nations.* Baltimore: The Johns Hopkins Press, 1961
Wilcox, Francis O., *Proposals for Changes in the United Nations.* Washington: The Brookings Institution, 1955
World Peace through the Rule of Law. Working Paper for the First World Conference, Athens, Greece, June 30-July 6, 1963.
Wortley, Ben Atkinson (ed.), *The United Nations, The First Ten Years.* Manchester: Manchester University Press, 1957
Wright, Quincy, *International Law and the United Nations.* London: Asia Publishing House, 1960

PUBLICATIONS

STUDIES

French Planning, *Vera Lutz*—1965

The Free Society, *Clare E. Griffin*—1965, 138 pp. ($4.50)

Congress and the Federal Budget, *Murray L. Weidenbaum* and *John S. Saloma III*—1965, 209 pp. ($4.00)

Poverty: Definition and Perspective, *Rose D. Friedman*—1965

The Responsible Use of Power: A Critical Analysis of the Congressional Budget Process, *John S. Saloma III*—1964

Federal Budgeting—the Choice of Government Programs, *Murray L. Weidenbaum*—1964

The Rural Electrification Administration—An Evaluation, *John D. Garwood* and *W. C. Tuthill*—1963

The Economic Analysis of Labor Union Power, Revised Edition, *Edward H. Chamberlin*—1963

United States Aid to Yugoslavia and Poland—Analysis of a Controversy, *Milorad M. Drachkovitch*—1963

Communists in Coalition Governments, *Gerhart Niemeyer*—1963

Subsidized Food Consumption, *Don Paarlberg*—1963

Automation—The Impact of Technological Change, *Yale Brozen*—1963

Essay on Apportionment and Representative Government, *Alfred de Grazia*—1963 ($2.00)

American Foreign Aid Doctrines, *Edward C. Banfield*—1963

The Rescue of the Dollar, *Wilson E. Schmidt*—1963

The Role of Gold, *Arthur Kemp*—1963

Pricing Power and "Administrative" Inflation—Concepts, Facts and Policy Implications, *Henry W. Briefs*—1962

Depreciation Reform and Capital Replacement, *William T. Hogan*—1962

The Federal Antitrust Laws, *Jerrold G. Van Cise*—1962

Consolidated Grants: A Means of Maintaining Fiscal Responsibility, *George C. S. Benson* and *Harold M. McClelland*—1961

Inflation: Its Causes and Cures, Revised and Enlarged Edition, *Gottfried Haberler*—1961

The Patchwork History of Foreign Aid, *Lorna Morley* and *Felix Morley*—1961

U.S. Immigration Policy and World Population Problems, *Virgil Salera*—1960

Voluntary Health Insurance in the United States, *Rita R. Campbell* and *W. Glenn Campbell*—1960

Unionism Reappraised: From Classical Unionism to Union Establishment, *Goetz Briefs*—1960

United States Aid and Indian Economic Development, *P. T. Bauer*—1959

Improving National Transportation Policy, *John H. Frederick*—1959

The Question of Governmental Oil Import Restrictions, *William H. Peterson*—1959

Labor Unions and the Concept of Public Service, *Roscoe Pound*—1959

Labor Unions and Public Policy, *Edward H. Chamberlin, Philip D. Bradley, Gerard D. Reilly,* and *Roscoe Pound*—1958, 177 pp. ($2.00)

115

116

Agricultural Surpluses and Export Policy, *Raymond F. Mikesell*—1958

Post-War West German and United Kingdom Recovery, *David McCord Wright*—1957

The Regulation of Natural Gas, *James W. McKie*—1957

Legal Immunities of Labor Unions, *Roscoe Pound*—1957

*Automation—Its Impact on Economic Growth and Stability, *Almarin Phillips* —1957

*Involuntary Participation in Unionism, *Philip D. Bradley*—1956

The Role of Government in Developing Peaceful Uses of Atomic Energy, *Arthur Kemp*—1956

The Role of The Federal Government in Housing, *Paul F. Wendt*—1956

The Upper Colorado Reclamation Project, Pro by *Sen. Arthur V. Watkins*, Con by *Raymond Moley*—1956

*Federal Aid to Education — Boon or Bane? *Roger A. Freeman*—1955

States Rights and the Law of Labor Relations, *Gerard D. Reilly*—1955

Three Taft-Hartley Issues: Secondary Boycotts, "Mandatory" Injunctions, Replaced Strikers' Votes, *Theodore R. Iserman*—1955

What Price Federal Reclamation? *Raymond Moley* — 1955

Private Investments Abroad, *Charles R. Carroll*—1954

Farm Price Supports—Rigid or Flexible, *Karl Brandt*—1954

*Currency Convertibility, *Gottfried Haberler*—1954

*The Control of the Location of Industry in Great Britain, *John Jewkes*—1952

*The Walsh-Healey Public Contracts Act, *John W. Van Sickle*—1952

The Economics of Full Employment: An Analysis of the U.N. Report on National and International Measures for Full Employment, *Wilhelm Röpke* —1952

Price Fixing for Foodstuffs, *Earl L. Butz*—1951

Manpower Needs and the Labor Supply, *Clarence D. Long*—1951

*An Economic Approach to Antitrust Problems, *Clare E. Griffin*—1951

*Valley Authorities, *Raymond Moley* —1950

*Farm Price and Income Supports, *O. B. Jesness*—1950

*Monetary Policy and Economic Prosperity: Testimony of Dr. W. W. Stewart (July 3-4, 1930) before the Macmillan Committee; with introduction by *Donald B. Woodward*—1950

*Corporate Profits in Perspective, *John Linter*—1949

*Current Problems of Immigration Policy, *E. P. Hutchinson*—1949

Guaranteed Employment and Wage Plans. A Summary and Critique of the Latimer Report and Related Documents, *William A. Berridge* and *Cedric Wolfe*—1948

The Foreign Loan Policy of the United States, *J. B. Condliffe*—1947

*Proposals for Consideration by an International Conference on Trade and Employment—*J. B. Condliffe*—1946

The Market for Risk Capital, *Jules I. Bogen*—1946

Unless otherwise shown in listing, Studies 1953 and earlier, 50 cents each; 1954 to date, $1.00 each.

* Out of Print

LEGISLATIVE AND SPECIAL ANALYSES

88th Congress, Second Session, 1964

Tax Proposals and the Federal Finances: Part V: Changes in the Proposed Revenue Act of 1964 Recommended by the Senate Committee on Finance. *Special Analysis*

Analysis of the Fiscal 1965 Federal Budget

The Panama Canal — Its Past and Future

The Federal Government in Behavioral Science: Fields, Methods, and Funds. *Special Analysis*

The Economic Opportunity Bill. Bills by *Sen. McNamara; Rep. Landrum*

Urban Mass Transportation Aid Bills. Bills by *Sen. Williams; Rep. Rains*

The Revised "War on Poverty" Bill. Bill by *Rep. Landrum*

Social Security Amendments of 1964. Bill by *Rep. Mills*

Presidental Disability and Vice-Presidential Vacancies

The Housing Act of 1964. Bill by *Sen. Sparkman*

Proposals Relating to Reapportionment of State Legislatures and The U.S. House of Representatives

The Drug Safety Problem. *Special Analysis*

89th Congress, First Session, 1965

The Appalachian Regional Development. Bills by *Sen. Randolph; Rep. Fallon*

The Gold Cover Bill. Bills by *Sen. Robertson; Rep. Patman*

Legislative History (88th Congress, 2d Session) and Index of AEI Publications

Proposals to Provide Federal Aid to Elementary and Secondary Schools. Bills by *Sen. Morse; Rep. Perkins*

Social Security Amendments of 1965. Bill by *Rep. Mills*

Analysis of the Fiscal 1966 Federal Budget

The Higher Education Bill of 1965. Bills by *Sen. Morse; Rep. Powell*

Housing and Urban Development Bills. Bills by *Sen. Sparkman* (by request); *Rep. Patman, Rep. Widnall*

The Excise Tax Reduction Bill. Bill by *Rep. Mills*